CHRISTM

A MASTER FILE
FOR CHILDREN 5 - 12

Compiled by
D C Perkins, BA (Hons), MEd, PhD (Wales) and E J Perkins, BSc (Hons), MEd
Illustrations by Craig Hildrew

THE CHRISTMAS MASTER FILE is full of ideas to help make learning fun. Compiled by experienced teachers, this is about a traditional Christmas in a modern world. The file satisfies the main concepts of the National Curriculum. The way in which the material is used depends on the age and ability of the children (and the time available). We hope you have as much fun using the file as **we have had writing it.**

D C and E J P

DOMINO BOOKS (WALES) LTD
SWANSEA SA1 1 FN
Tel. 01792 459378   Fax. 01792 466337
Christmas Master File © E J P & D C P 1993   ISBN 1 85772 065 2
Reprinted 1995, 1996, 1997

CONTENTS

The Nativity Play may be read or performed. Its length may be changed by selecting the acts and by including carols. There are opportunities for varying the number of children taking part. For example, the inclusion of a choir to sing carols, varying the number of 'extras', having children take the parts of the animals (sheep, donkey, camel . . .), having more than one narrator. Suggestions for costumes are shown in the illustrations in the text and also on page 73.

CONTENTS

The Nativity Play may be read or performed. Its length may be changed by the amount and by including carols. There are opportunities for varying the number of children taking part. For example, the inclusion of a choir to sing carols, varying the number of extras, having children take the parts of the animals (sheep, donkey, camel...), having more than one narrator. Suggestions for costumes are shown in the illustrations in the text and also on page 47

INTRODUCTION

This **Christmas Project File** has been specially designed to be used with children aged between 5 and 12. Themes and associated activities used to explain and illustrate the Christmas message-include

Arts and Crafts	Making Models
Comparative Religion	Maths
Cookery	Needlework
Drawing	Playing Games
Geography	Play Reading and Drama
Handwriting	Reading
History	Religious Studies
Language	Science
Literature	Solving Puzzles

The book is teacher-led and cross curricular. Older children will be able to follow the text with little help. Younger ones will enjoy the many pictures to colour, simple things to make and the Christmas stories. The way in which the book is used, how much 'listen, look and copy me' is needed depends on the ages and abilities of the pupils. The material may be adapted and extended to suit personal teacher needs.

As always, the selection of topics for a book is difficult and the compilers welcome comments and suggestions for future editions.

CHRISTMAS

THE CHRISTMAS MESSAGE

MARY'S SPECIAL VISITOR

Mary was a young girl who lived a long time ago in a town called Nazareth. She was soon going to marry a carpenter, Joseph.

One day when she was busy in her house, she heard a voice. She looked up and saw an angel. At first she was very frightened but the angel told her not to be afraid. He had come with a special message from God.

This made Mary even more alarmed. Why would God want to send a message to a poor girl like her?

The angel told Mary that she was going to have a baby, a son and that she should name the child Jesus, which means 'God saves'.

Mary did not really believe the angel but she could not forget him or his message.

THE CHRISTMAS MESSAGE

MARY'S SPECIAL VISITOR

Mary was a young girl who lived a long time ago in a town called Nazareth. She was soon going to marry a carpenter, Joseph.

One day when she was busy in her house, she heard a voice. She looked up and saw an angel. At first she was very frightened but the angel told her not to be afraid. He had come with a special message from God.

This made Mary even more alarmed. Why would God want to send a message to a poor girl like her?

The angel told Mary that she was going to have a baby, a son and that she should name the child Jesus, which means 'God saves'.

Mary did not really believe the angel but she could not forget him or his message.

An angel visited Mary with a message from God.

An angel visited Mary with a message from God

THE LONG JOURNEY TO BETHLEHEM

Joseph was surprised when he heard that Mary was going to have a baby but he decided that they should get married as they had planned.

At this time, the Roman Emperor, Augustus, commanded that everyone should go back to their home towns to register. He wanted to know how many people there were. This meant that Mary and Joseph had to go to Bethlehem where Joseph had been born.

Mary rode on a little donkey and Joseph walked beside her but the journey seemed very long. At night they slept on the ground wrapped only in their cloaks.

Mary was so tired that she nearly fell off the donkey.

After nearly a week they arrived in Bethlehem and Joseph tried to find a room for them. The baby was nearly ready to be born and he wanted somewhere safe for Mary and the child.

So many people had come back to Bethlehem to register that everywhere was full. There was not an empty room to be found.

Mary and Joseph were exhausted and did not know what to do.

THE LONG JOURNEY TO BETHLEHEM

Joseph was surprised when he heard that Mary was going to have a baby but he decided that they should get married as they had planned.

At this time, the Roman Emperor, Augustus, commanded that everyone should go back to their home towns to register. He wanted to know how many people there were. This meant that Mary and Joseph had to go to Bethlehem where Joseph had been born.

Mary rode on a little donkey and Joseph walked beside her but the journey seemed very long. At night they slept on the ground wrapped only in their cloaks.

Mary was so tired that she nearly fell off the donkey.

After nearly a week they arrived in Bethlehem and Joseph tried to find a room for them. The baby was nearly ready to be born and he wanted somewhere safe for Mary and the child.

So many people had come back to Bethlehem to register that everywhere was full. There was not an empty room to be found.

Mary and Joseph were exhausted and did not know what to do.

For Mary and Joseph, the journey to Bethlehem was long and tiring.

LOOKING FOR SHELTER

Because so many people had come to Bethlehem to register at the command of Emperor Augustus every room was full.

At last Mary and Joseph came to an inn and without much hope, Joseph knocked on the door. The innkeeper half opened the door and said that he did not have any accommodation for them. His inn was completely full and the only space left was in the stables with the animals, not really suitable for them.

In her condition, your wife needs a comfortable room to rest. A stable is no good at all, he said.

Joseph looked at Mary who was so tired. She nodded. *My wife can't travel any further. Please let us have the stable,* he begged.

Very well, said the innkeeper and reluctantly led the couple to the stables.

Joseph made Mary as comfortable as possible on some bales of hay and she fell asleep.

Much later the innkeeper heard the cries of a baby.

Jesus had been born.

LOOKING FOR SHELTER

Because so many people had come to Bethlehem to register at the command of Emperor Augustus every room was full.

At last Mary and Joseph came to an inn and without much hope, Joseph knocked on the door. The innkeeper half opened the door and said that he did not have any accommodation for them. His inn was completely full and the only space left was in the stables with the animals, not really suitable for them.

'In her condition, your wife needs a comfortable room to rest. A stable is no good at all,' he said.

Joseph looked at Mary, he was so tired. 'She could help, we can't travel much further. Please let us have the stable,' he begged.

'Very well,' said the innkeeper and reluctantly led the couple to the stables.

Joseph made Mary as comfortable as possible on some bales of hay and she fell asleep.

A little later the innkeeper heard the cries of a baby.

Jesus had been born.

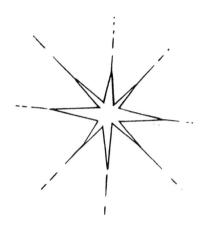

Jesus was born in a stable.

THE SHEPHERDS' STORY

The shepherds on the hillside outside the little town of Bethlehem warmed themselves at a fire they had made. Suddenly the quiet night sky was a blaze of light and the shining figure of an angel bent over them.

At first the shepherds were terrified but the angel said,
Don't be frightened. I have good news for you which will bring joy to the whole world. This very day a baby was born in Bethlehem. He is Christ the Lord! Go and see Him for yourselves. You will find Him lying in a manger.

The air filled with the sound of angels singing a hymn of praise and thankfulness to God. Then, as suddenly as they had come, the angels disappeared and the sky was black and silent again.

The shepherds did not know what to believe. *Come on,* they said. *Let's go and find out if it's true.* They hurried across the fields toward the sleeping town. When they found Joseph and Mary and saw the baby lying in the manger, they fell on their knees. Then they told Joseph and Mary all that had happened and the message that the angel had brought to them.

THE SHEPHERDS' STORY

The shepherds on the hillside outside the little town of Bethlehem warmed themselves at a fire they had made. Suddenly the quiet night sky was a blaze of light and the shining figure of an angel bent over them.

At first the shepherds were terrified but the angel said, 'Don't be frightened. I have good news for you which will bring joy to the whole world. This very day a baby was born in Bethlehem. He is Christ the Lord. Go and see Him for yourselves. You will find Him lying in a manger.'

The air filled with the sound of angels singing a hymn of praise and thankfulness to God. Then, as suddenly as they had come, the angels disappeared and the sky was black and silent again.

The shepherds did not know what to believe. 'Come on,' they said, 'Let's go and find out if it's true.' They hurried across the fields toward the sleeping town. When they found Joseph and Mary and saw the baby lying in the manger, they fell on their knees. Then they told Joseph and Mary all that had happened and the message that the angel had brought to them.

The shepherds visited the baby Jesus.

PRESENTS FIT FOR A KING

Everyone was waiting for the great king who God promised would come to rule the world in peace. One night some astrologers, wise men from the east, discovered a very bright star in the sky. They believed this was a sign that the king had been born.

Three of these wise men from the east packed their bags and set off with their camels towards the land of Israel. They made their way to the palace in Jerusalem, the capital city. They thought this was the most likely place where the new king would be born. At the palace, Herod the King, was very angry at the news that there was a new king who might take his throne from him. He told the travellers to go to Bethlehem.

Night fell as the wise men set off on their journey and once more they followed the star. When they found the baby Jesus they were surprised to find that there were no servants to look after the infant and his mother. There was only a simple peasant girl nursing her baby. But they were certain that they had found the long-promised king. They knelt down on the bare floor beside the cot of straw.

Then they offered the gifts they had brought with them. There was gold, a gift fit for a king. Next there was frankincense, the sweet-smelling incense offered in worship in the temples and lastly there was myrrh. Mary thought myrrh was a strange gift because it was the fragrant spice used when burying the dead.

PRESENTS FIT FOR A KING

Everyone was waiting for the great king, who God promised would come to rule the world in peace. One night some astrologers, wise men from the east, discovered a very bright star in the sky. They believed this was a sign that the king had been born.

Three of these wise men from the east packed their bags and set off with their camels towards the land of Israel. They made their way to the palace in Jerusalem, the capital city. They thought this was the most likely place where the new king would be born. At the palace, Herod the King, was very angry at the news that there was a new king who might take his throne from him. He told the travellers to go to Bethlehem.

Night fell as the travellers set off on their journey and once more they followed the star. When they found the baby Jesus they were surprised to find that there were no servants to look after the infant and his mother. There was only a simple peasant girl nursing her baby. But they were certain that they had found the long-promised king. They knelt down on the bare floor beside the cot of straw.

Then they offered the gifts they had brought with them. There was gold, a gift fit for a king. Next there was frankincense, the sweet-smelling incense offered in worship in the temples and lastly there was myrrh. Mary thought myrrh was a strange gift because it was the fragrant spice used when burying the dead.

The three wise men from the East brought gifts for Jesus.

The three wise men from the East brought gifts for Jesus.

A NATIVITY PLAY TO READ AND PERFORM

THE STORY OF CHRISTMAS

SCENE 1
MARY'S VISITOR

The scene is set in Mary's home. Mary, sitting on a chair slightly right of centre stage, is putting the finishing touches to her wedding dress.

PLAYERS   NARRATOR
MARY
THE ANGEL GABRIEL

COSTUME   TRADITIONAL
The clothes are simple and sandals are worn over bare feet.
The narrator who will be heard more clearly if he or she sits or stands to the front and side of the stage should also wear traditional clothing.

NARRATOR   This is a story that happened a long time ago, nearly two thousand years have passed but it is important that people all over the world remember it at Christmas time.
Mary was a young girl who lived with her parents Joachim and Anna in a little town called Nazareth. She was engaged to marry Joseph, a carpenter. Joseph and Mary were cousins and could trace their family back to King David.
One day when Mary was alone she had a special visitor.

The Angel Gabriel enters quietly from the left.

GABRIEL   Greetings, Mary.

MARY   *(Mary is startled and looks up, frightened.)* Who are you?

GABRIEL   Don't be afraid, Mary. I come with a message from God.

MARY   (Stands up, obviously puzzled). A message from God? You must have the wrong house. God would not want to bother with someone like me.

GABRIEL   (Smiling) No. The message is for you. I have good news for you. God is going to give you a baby.

MARY   That is impossible. I am not even married yet. Excuse me, but you must have lost your way. The message cannot be for me. Who are you anyway?

A NATIVITY PLAY TO READ AND PERFORM

THE STORY OF CHRISTMAS

SCENE 1
MARY'S VISITOR

The scene is set in Mary's home. Mary, sitting on a chair, stitching light-coloured, sitting on a chair centre stage, is putting the finishing touches to her wedding dress.

PLAYERS	NARRATOR
	MARY
	THE ANGEL GABRIEL

COSTUME	TRADITIONAL

The clothes are simple and sandals are worn over bare feet.
The narrator will be heard more clearly if he or she sits or stands to the front and side of the stage also wear traditional clothing.

NARRATOR   This is a story that happened a long time ago, nearly two thousand years have passed but it is important that people all over the world remember it at Christmas time.

Mary was a young girl who lived with her parents Joachim and Anna in a little town called Nazareth. She was engaged to marry Joseph, a carpenter. Joseph and Mary were cousins and could trace their family back to King David.

One day when Mary was alone she had a special visitor.

The Angel Gabriel enters quietly from the left.

GABRIEL   Greetings, Mary.

MARY   (Mary is startled and looks up, frightened.) Who are you?

GABRIEL   Don't be afraid, Mary. I come with a message from God.

MARY   (Stands up, obviously puzzled.) A message from God? You must have the wrong house. God would not want to bother with someone like me.

GABRIEL   (Smiling.) No. The message is for you. I have good news for you. God is going to give you a baby.

MARY   That is impossible. I am not even married yet. Excuse me, but you must have lost your way. The message cannot be for me. Who are you anyway?

GABRIEL   I am the Angel Gabriel. Mary, this is a very special baby.

MARY   *(Kneels in front of the angel.)* Sir, this is very hard to understand.

GABRIEL   God has chosen you to be the mother of His Son. When He is born
            you must call him Jesus. He will be great and His reign will never end.
            Goodbye Mary. *(Gabriel raises his hand as though blessing Mary and
            leaves the stage.)*

MARY   *(Getting up and facing the audience.)* Jesus means 'God saves'.

SCENE 2
JOSEPH'S DREAM

The scene is set in Joseph's workshop. There is a bench with a few tools. Joseph is talking to a friend.

PLAYERS	JOSEPH A FRIEND, PETER AN ANGEL
NARRATOR	When Mary told Joseph about the message from the Angel Gabriel he was puzzled, even a little scared. He loved Mary but marrying someone who was going to give birth to the Son of God was a big responsibility.
JOSEPH	I love Mary dearly but it's not quite what I expected. How can I be sure that she hasn't got another boy friend?
PETER	Mary definitely does not. I'm sure. She loves only you, Joseph. You must marry her. You're promised to each other and it would break her heart.
JOSEPH	I know. I'm so tired of worrying about it that I don't know what's right any more.
PETER	Why not sleep on it? I always find I can think more clearly in the morning.
JOSEPH	Perhaps you're right. I do love her.
PETER	And she loves you. Goodnight my friend. Sweet dreams.

Peter leaves the stage. Joseph wraps his cloak around him and lies down on the floor to sleep just to the right of centre stage. An angel enters from the left and stands a little away from Joseph.

ANGEL	Joseph.

Joseph stirs in his sleep but does not answer.

ANGEL	*(More loudly)* Joseph.
JOSEPH	Yes? Go away. I want to sleep. Leave me alone.
ANGEL	Just listen for a moment.
JOSEPH	*(Still lying on the floor as if sleeping).* Will you promise to go away then?
ANGEL	It's important that you marry Mary.
JOSEPH	She says she's going to have a baby and I don't think I'm ready for that yet. It's not fair on a chap.

SCENE 2
JOSEPH'S DREAM

The scene is set in Joseph's workshop. There is a bench with a few tools. Joseph is talking to a friend.

PLAYERS   JOSEPH
           A FRIEND, PETER
           AN ANGEL

NARRATOR   When Mary told Joseph about the message from the Angel Gabriel, he was puzzled, even a little scared. He loved Mary but marrying someone who was going to give birth to the Son of God was a big responsibility.

JOSEPH   I love Mary dearly but it's not quite what I expected. How can I be sure that she hasn't got another boy friend?

PETER   Mary definitely does not, I'm sure. She loves only you, Joseph. You must marry her. Ó you're promised to each other and it would break her heart.

JOSEPH   I know. I'm so tired of worrying about it that I don't know what's right any more.

PETER   Why not sleep on it? I always find I can think more clearly in the morning.

JOSEPH   Perhaps you're right. I do love her.

PETER   And she loves you. Goodnight my friend. Sweet dreams.

Peter leaves the stage. Joseph wraps his cloak around him and lies down on the floor to sleep just to the right of centre stage. An angel enters from the left and stands a little away from Joseph.

ANGEL   Joseph.

Joseph stirs in his sleep but does not answer.

ANGEL   (More loudly) Joseph.

JOSEPH   Yes? Go away. I want to sleep. Leave me alone.

ANGEL   Just listen for a moment.

JOSEPH   (Still lying on the floor at if sleeping) Will you promise to go away then?

ANGEL   It's important that you marry Mary.

JOSEPH   She says she's going to have a baby and I don't think I'm ready for that yet. It's not fair on a chap.

ANGEL	*(Smiling.)* Mary is a very special person and the baby is the Son of God. He is a gift from God. He will carry out God's work and save people from their sins.
JOSEPH	Why Mary, why us?
ANGEL	It is God's will. The baby will be called Jesus. He and Mary need you to look after them.

Angel exits from the left. Joseph continues to sleep and the light on the stage goes out. (If possible leave a light on the narrator.)

NARRATOR	So Mary and Joseph were married with the usual fuss. Everyone said Mary was beautiful and Joseph was lucky to get her and that Joseph was very handsome and would make an excellent husband. Soon Mary knew she was going to have a baby. She and Joseph were very happy.

ANGEL   (Smiling.) Mary is a very special person and the baby is the Son of God. He is a gift from God. He will carry out God's work and save people from their sins.

JOSEPH   Why Mary, why us?

ANGEL   It is God's will. The baby will be called Jesus. He and Mary need you to look after them.

Angel exits from the left. Joseph continues to sleep and the light on the stage goes out. (If possible leave a light on the narrator.)

NARRATOR   So Mary and Joseph were married with the usual fuss. Everyone said Mary was beautiful and Joseph was lucky to get her and that Joseph was very handsome and would make an excellent husband. Soon Mary knew she was going to have a baby. She and Joseph were very happy.

SCENE 3
BORN IN A STABLE

The scene is set in the stables and the courtyard of an inn. Most of the stage to the right is the stable with several bales of hay. To the left is the courtyard.

PLAYERS   NARRATOR
                    MARY
                    JOSEPH
                    INNKEEPER

NARRATOR   At this time, the Roman Emperor Augustus decided to hold a census, that is to write the names of everyone who lived in his country on a register. He did not want to miss anyone off the register and he did not want anyone to be entered twice so he ordered everyone to go back to the town where they had been born. Joseph had to go to Bethlehem. Mary could have stayed in Nazareth but she decided that she wanted her son to be born in Bethlehem. Mary rode on a small donkey and Joseph walked beside her. They walked for days and slept at night on the ground with their cloaks wrapped around them.

MARY   *(Mary's tummy is padded to show she is pregnant.)* I can't believe that Bethlehem is so full.

JOSEPH   It's this wretched census. Everyone's come home and all the rooms are taken.

MARY   (Leans on Joseph's arm.) We must find somewhere soon, I'm so tired. This journey is so unfair.

JOSEPH   It's the same for everyone. The Emperor said that we all had to go back to our homelands.

They walk slowly towards the door of the inn.

JOSEPH   We'll try this inn. Perhaps they'll have something.

Joseph knocks on the door and the Innkeeper half opens the door.

INNKEEPER   We're full up. All the rooms are taken.

He shuts the door and Joseph knocks again.

INNKEEPER   Be off with you. There's no room. It's not my fault. I'm sick of turning people away.

JOSEPH   I'm sorry to bother you. It's just that we have been travelling for so long and my wife is exhausted. We're looking for somewhere to rest awhile.

The Innkeeper opens the door and looks more closely at Mary.

SCENE 3
BORN IN A STABLE

The scene is set in the stables and the courtyard of an inn. Most of the stage to the right is the stable with several bales of hay. To the left is the courtyard.

PLAYERS   NARRATOR
           MARY
           JOSEPH
           INNKEEPER

NARRATOR   At this time, the Roman Emperor Augustus decided to hold a census, that is to write the names of everyone who lived in his country on a register. He did not want to miss anyone off the register and he did not want anyone to be entered twice so he ordered everyone to go back to the town where they had been born. Joseph had to go to Bethlehem. Mary could have stayed in Nazareth but she decided that she wanted her son to be born in Bethlehem. Mary rode on a small donkey and Joseph walked beside her. They walked for days and slept at night on the ground with their cloaks wrapped around them.

MARY   (Mary's tummy is padded out since she is pregnant.) I can't believe that Bethlehem is so far!

JOSEPH   It's this wretched census. Everyone's going home and all the rooms are taken.

MARY   (Leans on Joseph's arm.) We must find somewhere soon. I'm so tired. This journey is so unfair.

JOSEPH   It's the same for everyone. The Emperor said that we all had to go back to our homelands.

They walk slowly towards the door of the inn.

JOSEPH   We'll try this inn. Perhaps they'll have something.

Joseph knocks on the door and the innkeeper half opens the door.

INNKEEPER   We're full up. All the rooms are taken.

He slams the door and Joseph knocks again.

INNKEEPER   Be off with you. There's no room. It's not my fault. I'm sick of turning people away.

JOSEPH   I'm sorry to bother you. It's just that we have been travelling for so long and my wife is exhausted. We're looking for somewhere to rest awhile.

The innkeeper opens the door and looks more closely at Mary.

INNKEEPER   She should not be travelling in her condition.
He starts to turn away and close the door again then stops.
            You could rest in the stable but it's no place to have a baby.

MARY   Thank you. It's not due yet. *(She pats her tummy.)*

INNKEEPER   I'm glad to hear it. (He leads them to the stable.)

MARY   Oh Thank you. This will be fine. If we could just rest for a while.

INNKEEPER   Very well. But there are no doctors here if your baby comes.

The Innkeeper leaves the stage and Joseph makes Mary comfortable on a bale of hay. She falls asleep almost immediately.

NARRATOR   Later, the baby Jesus was born. Mary wrapped him in swaddling clothes and put him to sleep in a manger.

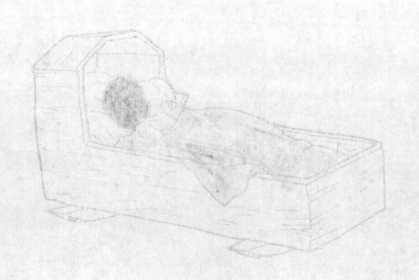

SCENE 4
THE SHEPHERDS' STORY

The scene is set in the courtyard of the inn and then in the stable. The baby Jesus is lying in a cradle lined with straw.

PLAYERS   THREE SHEPHERDS, MATTHEW, ISAAC AND BENJAMIN
                   INNKEEPER
                   JOSEPH
                   MARY
                   NARRATOR

Three shepherds enter the courtyard talking loudly.

MATTHEW   We've looked everywhere. It must have been our imagination.

ISAAC   We all saw it. The bright light, the angel. Unless we're all mad. Watch what you're doing with the lantern. You'll set us all on fire.

BENJAMIN   *(Straightening the lantern which he had nearly dropped.)* Speak for yourself. We all heard the message and we all heard the angels singing. There's got to be a baby somewhere.

MATTHEW   The angel said to follow the star and we have.

ISAAC   All we want now is to find a manger with a baby in it.

Innkeeper opens the door. Very angry.

INNKEEPER   What's all the noise about? You'll wake all my guests and I have enough trouble as it is with this new baby in the stable. I told them it wasn't fit but they wouldn't listen.

The three shepherds catch hold of the innkeeper.

SHEPHERDS   *(all together)* Baby? What baby? Where is he?

INNKEEPER   *(pulling himself free and tidying his clothes.)* The one that's just been born in the stable.

The three shepherds rush to the stable then stop, nearly falling over each other as they see the sleeping infant.

BENJAMIN   It's really true. It's really true.

Mary is resting and Joseph is watching over her and the child. The baby cries as Benjamin pushes himself to the front. Joseph looks at the shepherds.

JOSEPH   What's true? Who are you? What do you want?

MATTHEW   We had a message from an angel.

SCENE 4
THE SHEPHERDS' STORY

The scene is set in the stable, inside the inn and in the stable. The baby Jesus is lying in a cradle lined with straw.

PLAYERS   THREE SHEPHERDS, MATTHEW, ISAAC AND BENJAMIN
INNKEEPER
JOSEPH
MARY
NARRATOR

Three shepherds enter the stage and talking loudly.

MATTHEW   We've looked everywhere. It must have been our imagination.

ISAAC   We all saw it. The bright light, the angel. Unless we're all mad. Watch what you're doing with the lantern. You'll set us all on fire.

BENJAMIN   (Straightening the lantern which he had nearly dropped.) Speak for yourself. We all heard the message and we all heard the angels singing. There's got to be a baby somewhere.

MATTHEW   The angel said to follow the star and we have.

ISAAC   All we want now is to find a manger with a baby in it.

Innkeeper opens the door. Very angry.

INNKEEPER   What's all the noise about? You'll wake all my guests and I have enough trouble as it is with this new baby in the stable. I told them it wasn't fit but they wouldn't listen.

The three shepherds catch hold of the innkeeper.

SHEPHERDS   (all together) Baby? What baby? Where is he?

INNKEEPER   (pulling himself free and drying his clothes.) The one that's just been born in the stable.

The three shepherds rush to the stable, then stop, nearly falling over each other as they see the sleeping infant.

BENJAMIN   It's really true - it's really true

Mary is resting and Joseph is watching over her and the child. The baby cries as Benjamin makes his way to the front. Joseph looks at the shepherds.

JOSEPH   What's this? Who are you? What do you want?

MATTHEW   We had a message from an angel.

JOSEPH	The angels seem to have been very busy lately.
ISAAC	We were watching our sheep, we're shepherds, you know. *(He waves his shepherd's crook.)*
MATTHEW	Now see what you've done. You've woken the baby.
JOSEPH	Do you think you could put that lantern down before you set us all on fire?
BENJAMIN	Sorry. It's just that it's a miracle. Just like the angel said.
JOSEPH	What do you want? You're welcome to share the stable if that's any use.
ISAAC	We'd better explain. We came to see the baby.
MARY	Why? How did you know he had been born?
MATTHEW	I'll tell you what happened. We were sitting around the fire on the hillside . . .
BENJAMIN	It gets very cold at night. It's alright for the sheep, they've got thick woolly coats.
ISAAC	Quiet Benjamin. Go on Matthew.
MATTHEW	Suddenly there was a bright light all around us.
BENJAMIN	It started in the sky and sort of spread everywhere and then there were voices.
ISAAC	The light was really an angel.
BENJAMIN	We were frightened, at least I was.
MATTHEW	Benjamin will you please be quiet and keep still. The angel told us that a baby would be born today in Bethlehem and that He was Christ the Lord. He said we would find Him lying in a manger.
BENJAMIN	And we have. *(He leaned forward and gently stroked the baby's cheek.)* He's very beautiful.

The three shepherds kneel before the baby.

ISAAC	Now that we've seen Him for ourselves we can tell everyone about Him.
MARY	An angel came to see me too. He said that I would have a very special baby, the Son of God and that He would be called Jesus.
MATTHEW	I don't really understand what is going on but I think we shall tell everyone that the Son of God has been born.

The three shepherds leave.

SCENE 5

KING HEROD

The scene is set in Herod's palace. Herod is sitting on a throne in the centre of the stage surrounded by courtiers and slave girls.

PLAYERS   THE THREE WISE MEN, BALTHAZAR, CASPAR, MELCHIOR
                    HEROD
                    COURTIERS
                    SLAVE GIRLS
                    SERVANT
                    NARRATOR

NARRATOR   One night some astrologers, wise men from the east, discovered a very bright star in the sky. They believed this was a sign that the king everyone was waiting for had been born.
                    Three of these wise men packed their bags and set off with their camels towards the land of Israel. They made their way to the palace in Jerusalem, the capital city. They thought this was the most likely place where the new king would be born.

Enter a servant.

SERVANT   Sire, I have some news for you. *(He kneels in front of the King.)* I ask permission to speak.

HEROD   *(Raises his hand imperiously.)* Very well. Be brief. I am busy.

SERVANT   Three men from the east have arrived at the palace. They say they have some important news for you, a prophesy about a new king, a king who will reign in the future. *(The servant's voice trails away as Herod stands up in anger.)*

HEROD   What do you mean 'future king'? I am the king now and in the future.

SERVANT   They crave an audience with you sire.

HEROD   Do they indeed. Very well. Bring them to me. *(He dismisses the servant with a wave of his hand. The other players move to the sides of the stage. Herod then speaks to himself.)* I'd better listen to what they have to say. There'll be no future king except me if I have anything to do with it.

The servant leads the three travellers on to the stage. (If possible entry should be down an aisle in the middle or to the side of the audience.)

BALTHAZAR   It's very good of you to see us, sire. We've been travelling for a long time.

All three men bow low in front of the king.

HEROD   You are welcome. What is your business?

SCENES

KING HEROD

The scene is set in Herod's palace. Herod is sitting on a throne in the centre of the stage, surrounded by courtiers and slave girls.

PLAYERS   THE THREE WISE MEN, BALTHAZAR, CASPAR, MELCHIOR
    HEROD
    COURTIERS
    SLAVE GIRLS
    SERVANT
    NARRATOR

NARRATOR   One night some astrologers, wise men from the east, discovered a very bright star in the sky. They believed this was a sign that the king everyone was waiting for had been born.
Three of these wise men packed their bags and set off with their camels towards the land of Israel. They made their way to the palace in Jerusalem, the capital city. They thought this was the most likely place where the new King would be born.

Enter a servant

SERVANT   Sire, I have someone for you. (He kneels in front of the King) I ask permission to speak.

HEROD   (Rouses and looks impatiently) Very well. Be brief. I am busy.

SERVANT   Three men from the east have arrived at the palace. They say they have some important news for you, a prophecy about a new King, a King who will reign in the future. (The servant's voice trails away as Herod stands up in anger)

HEROD   What do you mean 'a new King'? I am the king now and in the future.

SERVANT   They crave an audience with you sire.

HEROD   Do they indeed. Very well. Bring them to me. (He dismisses the servant with a wave of his hand. The other players move to the sides of the stage. Herod then speaks to himself) I'd better listen to what they have to say. There'll be no future king except me if I have anything to do with it.

The servant leads the three travellers on to the stage. (If possible they should be down a circle in the middle or to the side of the audience.)

BALTHAZAR   It's very good of you to see us sire. We've been travelling for a long time.

All three men bow low in front of the king

HEROD   You are welcome. What is your errand?

MELCHIOR	We have been following a star in the heavens and it has led us here.
CASPAR	We believe that the star is a sign that a new king has been born. We came here because it seems the most likely place for Him to be born.
HEROD	I am king here. There is no other king.
BALTHAZAR	It is a sign sire. He has been born in Bethlehem. He is very important and we would like to see Him.
CASPAR	He will grow up to be more powerful than any man on earth. He will reign over the whole world forever.
HEROD	(Sarcastically) Really. I can hardly wait to meet Him.
CASPAR	He is to be the King of the Jews.
HEROD	Then He must be at Bethlehem. These Jews are always making trouble. If they have a king, they will be worse than ever. You have done right to tell me. I would like to know where this baby is.

The three wise men bow to Herod and leave the stage.

MELCHIOR   We have been following a star in the heavens and it has led us here.

CASPAR   We believe that the star is a sign that a new king has been born. We came here because it seems the most likely place for Him to be born.

HEROD   I am king here. There is no other king.

BALTHAZAR   It is a sign that He has been born in Bethlehem. He is very important and we would like to see Him.

CASPAR   He will grow up to be more powerful than any man on earth. He will reign over the whole world forever.

HEROD   (sarcastically) Really. I can hardly wait to meet Him.

CASPAR   He is to be the King of the Jews.

HEROD   Then He must be at Bethlehem. These Jews are always making trouble. If they have a king, they will be worse than ever. You have done right to tell me. I would like to know where this baby is.

The three wise men bow to Herod and leave the stage.

SCENE 6

THE THREE WISE MEN FROM THE EAST

The scene is set in the courtyard of the inn and then in the stable. The baby Jesus is lying in a cradle lined with straw.

PLAYERS   THE THREE WISE MEN, BALTHAZAR, CASPAR, MELCHIOR
                        JOSEPH
                        MARY
                        INNKEEPER
                        NARRATOR

NARRATOR   Night fell as the wise men set off on their journey and once more they followed the star.

The three wise men enter the courtyard.

CASPAR   I'm so tired. This must be the place.

INNKEEPER   More visitors. I suppose you want to see the baby as well?

BALTHAZAR   Of course. Where is he?

INNKEEPER   In the stable. I don't know what all the fuss is about. One baby is the same as any other. They all do the same things. Keep you awake at night with their crying. Always wanting to be fed or nursed. I don't know why women bother to have them.

MELCHIOR   This one is different. This is the Son of God.

INNKEEPER   Where have you come from?

CASPAR   From a country far to the East of here. We have been following a star for weeks.

INNKEEPER   Well come with me. I hope you think it 's been worth while.

The three men follow the innkeeper to the stable.

NARRATOR   They were surprised to find that there were no servants to look after the infant and his mother, none of the trappings associated with a royal birth. There was only a young woman nursing her baby. But they were certain that they had found the long-promised king.

They kneel on the bare floor beside the cot of straw.

MELCHIOR   We have brought gifts for the child. I have brought gold, a gift for a king.

Melchior places his gift on the floor at the foot of the cradle.

SCENE 6
THE THREE WISE MEN FROM THE EAST

The scene is set in the courtyard of the inn and then in the stable. The baby Jesus is lying in a cradle lined with straw.

PLAYERS   THE THREE WISE MEN, BALTHAZAR, CASPAR, MELCHIOR
JOSEPH
MARY
INNKEEPER
NARRATOR

NARRATOR   Night falls as the wise men set off on their journey and once more they followed the star.

The three wise men cross the courtyard.

CASPAR   I'm so tired. This must be the place.

INNKEEPER   More visitors. I suppose you want to see the baby as well?

BALTHAZAR   Of course. Where is he?

INNKEEPER   I don't see. I don't know what all the fuss is about. One baby is the same as any other. They all do the same things. Keep you awake at night with their crying. Always wanting to be fed or nursed. I don't know why women bother to have them.

MELCHIOR   This one is different. This is the Son of God.

INNKEEPER   Where have you come from?

CASPAR   From a country far to the East of here. We have been following a star for weeks.

INNKEEPER   Well come with me. I hope you think it's been worth while.

The three men follow the innkeeper to the stable.

NARRATOR   They were amazed to find that there were no servants to look after the infant and his mother, none of the trappings associated with a royal birth. There was only a young woman nursing her baby. But they were certain that they had found the long-promised king.

They knelt on the barn floor beside the tiny princes.

MELCHIOR   We have brought gifts for the child. These have brought gold, a gift for a king.

Melchior places gift at the feet of the son of Mary and the child.

CASPAR   I have brought frankincense, incense for a God.

Caspar places his gift to the side and front of the cradle.

BALTHAZAR   I have brought myrrh for the One who will bring a message of hope and peace to the world.

Balthazar places his gift beside Caspar's.

MELCHIOR   It's getting late, we must find somewhere to sleep.

MARY   Thank you for all these wonderful gifts.

INNKEEPER   I have a vacant room and I would be honoured if you would use it tonight.

The three wise men follow the innkeeper off stage.

JOSEPH   I think we should all go to sleep now.

CASPAR   I have brought frankincense, incense, for a God.

Caspar places his gift to the side and front of the cradle.

BALTHAZAR   I have brought myrrh for the One who will bring a message of hope and peace to the world.

Balthazar places his gift beside Caspar's.

MELCHIOR   It's getting late; we must find somewhere to sleep.

MARY   Thank you for all these wonderful gifts.

INNKEEPER   I have a vacant room and I would be honoured if you would use it tonight.

The three wise men follow the innkeeper off stage.

JOSEPH   I think we should all go to sleep now.

SCENE 7
THE WISE MEN'S DREAM

The scene is set in a room in the inn. The three wise men are asleep on the floor.

PLAYERS   THE THREE WISE MEN:
BALTHAZAR,
CASPAR,
MELCHIOR
NARRATOR

NARRATOR   The night has passed quickly for our friends but they have not slept undisturbed.

Balthazar stretches and yawns then gets up.
BALTHAZAR   It's time to wake up. Come on you two. We can make an early start. How did you sleep?

Balthazar shakes Melchior to wake him..

MELCHIOR   Fine. Anything would be comfortable after that camel ride.

Caspar sits up.

CASPAR   I wish you two would be quiet. I'm still tired. I didn't sleep all that well. In fact I had an odd dream.

BALTHAZAR   What kind of dream?

CASPAR   I dreamt that we should not go back to Herod to tell him about Jesus. In fact I think we should go home through Jerusalem.

BALTHAZAR   I had the same dream.

MELCHIOR   *(A little sheepishly)* Me too.

CASPAR   Why didn't you say so before?

MELCHIOR   I felt a little foolish about it but I agree with you . We will give Herod a wide berth.

CASPAR   Herod is a tyrant who will stop at nothing to keep power. He will kill any one who gets in his way.

BALTHAZAR   You think the baby might be in danger? So do I. We shall not go back to Herod to tell him about the Christ child.

MELCHIOR   We'll go when it is dark. Herod's spies will think that we did not find the baby.

SCENE 7

SCENE 8
THE WARNING TO JOSEPH

The scene is set in the stable. It is still night and Joseph wakes up.

PLAYERS   JOSEPH
                MARY
                NARRATOR

JOSEPH   Mary wake up.

MARY   What's the matter? I'm still tired and it's dark. go back to sleep.

JOSEPH   I'm worried. I had a dream. I heard a voice saying that we should go to Egypt. Herod is looking for the child and means to kill him.

Mary stands up at once. She is now wide awake and starts to wrap the baby in a shawl.

MARY   Let's go now. At once.

NARRATOR   In the dark, before the sun was up, Mary and Joseph slipped out of Bethlehem and began the long journey to Egypt where Jesus would be safe.

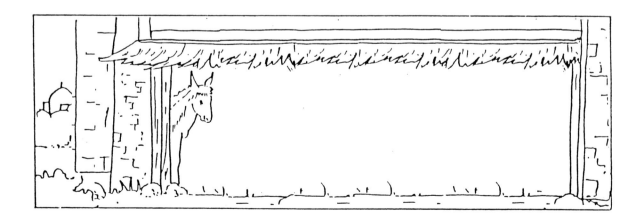

SCENE 9
THE HUNT FOR BABY JESUS

The scene is set in Herod's palace. Herod is striding up and down followed by an anxious servant wringing his hands. The king is very angry.

PLAYERS   HEROD
                 SERVANT
                 CAPTAIN OF THE GUARD
                 NARRATOR

HEROD   I should not have trusted them. I should have sent a spy after them.

SERVANT   Sire, perhaps they did not find this new king. Perhaps he does not exist.

Herods stops pacing and turns on the speaker.

HEROD   If you talk any more nonsense I will have your tongue cut out. Of course there's a new king. The palace is alive with rumour. They think I'm deaf and blind. I hear them whispering in corners. I see them laughing behind my back.

He continues pacing. The servant wisely keeps out of his way.

HEROD   It is now more than a year since those charlatans came here looking for the new king. I must find the child and kill him.

SERVANT   Sire, the soldiers have searched high and low. There are so many babies. They cannot tell one from the other.

HEROD   Exactly. We must kill them all.

SERVANT   You don't mean that sire. There must be thousands. We would have a Jewish uprising. The soldiers would not do it.

Herod becomes even more angry.

HEROD   *(Shouting and waving his arms.)* Bring me the Captain of the Guard. At once!

The servant leaves the stage and returns in a few minutes with the Captain. During this time Herod's mood suddenly changes. He smiles and rubs his hands with glee having found what he thinks is the perfect solution to his problem.

HEROD   *(Speaking to himself.)* Got it! Got it! The perfect solution. I knew I'd think of something if I kept at it long enough.

CAPTAIN   *(Bowing low.)* You sent for me, sire?

HEROD	*(Stands still in the centre of the stage, hands on hips.)* You know that there is talk of a new Messiah among the Jews. A child that will grow up to lead them. I want him killed.
CAPTAIN	We have tried to find him sire but without success.
HEROD	I am tired of waiting and sick of your incompetence. I have fresh orders for you. The child cannot be more than two years old. Take your men and kill every male child in the province of Judaea who is aged two years or less.

The servant and captain gasp in horror.

CAPTAIN	I'm not sure the men will do it. Such a massacre on such a scale of young innocents.

Herod walks up to the Captain and standing close to him, hisses with fury.

HEROD	If you will not carry out my orders I will have you put to death. That is enough. Return when the task is done.

The servant and captain exit. Herod sits on his throne.

Offstage can be heard shouts, howling and weeping.

NARRATOR	The land was plunged into despair as the soldiers carried out their orders.

The captain enters, dragging his feet, his head bowed. He kneels before Herod.

HEROD	Is the work complete?
CAPTAIN	*(In a sad dull voice.)* Yes. Every male child of two years or less is dead.

Herod struts across the stage and then stands in the centre, hands on hips, head high.

HEROD	The Jews have no king?
CAPTAIN	*(Bitterly)* The Jews have no king.
HEROD	Judaea has only one king.
CAPTAIN	Judaea has only one king.
HEROD	Good then that's the end of the matter.
NARRATOR	Mary and Joseph stayed in Egypt until Herod died. Then they returned to Mary's home town of Nazareth. Jesus grew up in the town where it all started with the visit of the angel of God to Mary. He grew into a strong, healthy young man whose faith and work were to save the whole world.

HEROD   (Stands but in the centre of the stage, hands on hips.) You know that there is talk of a new Messiah among the Jews. A child that will grow up to lead them. I want him killed.

CAPTAIN   We have tried to find him, sire, but without success.

HEROD   I am tired of waiting and sick of your incompetence. I have fresh orders for you. The child cannot be more than two years old. Take your men and kill every male child in the province of Judaea who is aged two years or less.

The servant and captain gasp in horror.

CAPTAIN   I'm not sure the men will do it. Such a massacre on such a scale of young innocents.

Herod walks up to the Captain and standing close to him, hisses with fury.

HEROD   If you will not carry out my orders I will have you put to death. That is enough. Return when the task is done.

The servant and captain exit. Herod sits on his throne.

(Strange sad lighting, loud wind and weeping.)

NARRATOR   The land was plunged into despair as the soldiers carried out their orders.

The captain enters, dragging his feet, his head bowed. He kneels before Herod.

HEROD   Is the work complete?

CAPTAIN   (In a sad dull voice.) Yes. Every male child of two years or less is dead.

Herod struts the stage and then stands centre stage, hands on hips, head high.

HEROD   The Jews have no king?

CAPTAIN   (Bitterly.) The Jews have no king.

HEROD   Judaea has only one King.

CAPTAIN   Judaea has only one king.

HEROD   Good then that's the end of the matter.

NARRATOR   Mary and Joseph stayed in Egypt until Herod died. Then they returned to Mary's home town of Nazareth. Jesus grew up in the town where it all started with the visit of the angel of God to Mary. He grew into a strong, healthy young man whose faith and work were to save the whole world.

CAROLS

At first the word 'carol' meant ring-dance, because early carollers danced round in a circle as they sang. Now carols are sung at Christmas but once they were sung at other times as well - Easter, May Day, Whitsuntide and other festivals.

Some carols tell a story, others are songs of celebration. Many of the carols sung today are at least 400 years old. Some formed part of the religious plays, called Mystery Plays, that were acted in those days at Whitsuntide or at Corpus Christi. Others were sung round the Christmas crib in churches or in large houses. Most were sung by parties of singers going from door to door, just as they are today.

A few old carols are not religious - they are secular (worldly) carols. One of the most famous secular carols is 'The Twelve Days of Christmas'. No one knows how old this is and it was probably written when the Christmas holiday lasted for 12 days from Christmas Eve to Twelfth Night. It is a cumulative or 'adding-on song' in which a new line is added to each verse.

CAROLS

At first the word 'carol' meant ring-dance, because early carollers danced round in a circle as they sang. Now carols are sung at Christmas but once they were sung at other times as well – Easter, May Day, Whitsuntide and other festivals.

Some carols tell a story, others are songs of celebration. Many of the carols sung today are at least 400 years old. Some formed part of the religious plays, called Mystery Plays, that were acted in those days at Whitsuntide or at Corpus Christi. Others were sung round the Christmas crib in churches or in large houses. Most were sung by parties of singers going from door to door just as they are today.

A few old carols are not religious – they are secular (worldly) carols. One of the most famous secular carols is The Twelve Days of Christmas. No one knows how old this is and it was probably written when the Christmas holiday lasted for 12 days from Christmas Eve to Twelfth Night. It is a cumulative or adding-on song, in which a new line is added to each verse.

CAROL SINGING

Singing carols is one of the nicest part of any Christmas celebration. These favourites may be sung between the scenes of the Nativity Play, as part of a Christmas service or on their own.

ONCE IN ROYAL DAVID'S CITY

1   Once in royal David's city
Stood a lowly cattle shed,
Where a mother laid her baby
In a manger for His bed.
Mary was that mother mild,
Jesus Christ, her little child.

2   He came down to earth from heaven
Who is God and Lord of all;
And His shelter was a stable,
And His cradle was a stall:
With the poor and meek and lowly
Lived on earth our saviour holy.

3   And through all His wondrous childhood
He would honour and obey,
Love, and watch the lowly maiden
In whose gentle arms He lay.
Christian children all must be
Mild, obedient, good as He.

4   For he is our childhood's pattern:
Day by day like us He grew;
He was little, weak, and helpless:
Tears and smiles like us He knew:
And He feeleth for our sadness,
And He shareth in our gladness.

5   And our eyes at last shall see Him,
Through His own redeeming love;
For that child so dear and gentle
Is our Lord in heaven above;
And He leads His children on
To the place where He is gone.

Cecil Frances Alexander, 1823 - 85

AWAY IN A MANGER

1   Away in a manger,
No crib for a bed,
The little Lord Jesus
Laid down His sweet head;
The stars in the bright sky
Looked down where He lay;
The little Lord Jesus
Asleep on the hay.

2   The cattle are lowing,
The baby awakes,
But little Lord Jesus
No crying he makes.
I love you, Lord Jesus:
Look down from on high
And stay by my side
Until morning is nigh.

3   Be near me, Lord Jesus.
I ask you to stay
Close by me forever
And love me I pray.
Bless all the dear children
In your tender care,
And fit us for heaven
To live with you there.

This carol may have been written by the German reformer, Martin Luther but is more likely to have been written by an American from Pennsylvania.

CAROL SINGING

Singing carols is one of the nicest part of any Christmas celebration. These favourites may be sung between the scenes of the Nativity Play, as part of a Christmas service or on their own.

ONCE IN ROYAL DAVID'S CITY

1. Once in royal David's city
Stood a lowly cattle shed,
Where a mother laid her baby
In a manger for His bed,
Mary was that mother mild,
Jesus Christ, her little child.

2. He came down to earth from heaven
Who is God and Lord of all,
And His shelter was a stable,
And His cradle was a stall;
With the poor and mean and lowly,
Lived on earth our Saviour holy.

3. And through all His wondrous childhood
He would honour and obey,
Love, and watch the lowly maiden,
In whose gentle arms He lay:
Christian children all must be
Mild, obedient, good as He.

4. For he is our childhood's pattern,
Day by day like us He grew;
He was little, weak, and helpless,
Tears and smiles like us He knew;
And He feeleth for our sadness,
And He shareth in our gladness.

5. And our eyes at last shall see Him,
Through His own redeeming love,
For that child so dear and gentle
Is our Lord in heaven above,
And He leads His children on
To the place where He is gone.

Cecil Frances Alexander, 1823 - 95

AWAY IN A MANGER

1. Away in a manger,
No crib for a bed,
The little Lord Jesus
Laid down His sweet head.
The stars in the bright sky
Looked down where He lay,
The little Lord Jesus
Asleep on the hay.

2. The cattle are lowing,
The baby awakes,
But little Lord Jesus
No crying He makes,
I love you, Lord Jesus!
Look down from on high,
And stay by my side,
Until morning is nigh.

3. Be near me, Lord Jesus,
I ask you to stay
Close by me forever,
And love me I pray.
Bless all the dear children
In your tender care,
And fit us for heaven,
To live with you there.

This carol may have been written by the German reformer, Martin Luther, but it is more likely to have been written by an American from Pennsylvania.

O COME ALL YE FAITHFUL

1   O come, all ye faithful,
    Joyful and triumphant.
    O come ye, O come ye
        to Bethlehem.
    Come and behold him,
    Born the king of angels.

    CHORUS
    O come let us adore him,
    O come let us adore him,
    O come let us adore him,
        Christ the Lord.

2   Sing choirs of angels,
        Sing in exultation.
    Sing, all ye citizens of heaven above
    'Glory to God in the highest.'

    CHORUS

3   Yea, Lord, we greet Thee,
        Born this happy morning;
    Jesus, to Thee be glory given,
        Word of the Father,
        Now in flesh appearing:

    CHORUS

IN THE BLEAK MID-WINTER

1   In the bleak mid-winter,
        Frosty wind made moan,
        Earth stood hard as iron,
        Water like a stone:
    Snow had fallen, snow on snow,
            Snow on snow,
        In the bleak mid-winter
            Long ago.

2   Our God, heaven cannot hold Him
        Nor earth sustain;
    Heaven and earth shall flee away
        When he comes to reign
        In the bleak mid-winter
        A stable-space sufficed
        The Lord God Almighty,
            Jesus Christ.

3   Angels and archangels
        May have gathered there,
        Cherubim and seraphim
            Thronged the air;
        But His mother only,
        In her maiden bliss,
    Worshipped the Beloved
            With a kiss.

4   What can I give Him,
            Poor as I am?
        If I were a shepherd,
        I would bring a lamb;
        If I were a wise man,
        I would do my part;
    Yet what I can I give Him -
            Give my heart.

Christina Georgina Rosetti, 1830 - 94

O COME ALL YE FAITHFUL

1. O come, all ye faithful,
joyful and triumphant,
O come ye, O come ye
to Bethlehem;
Come and behold him,
Born the King of angels.

CHORUS
O come let us adore him,
O come let us adore him,
O come let us adore him,
Christ the Lord.

2. Sing choirs of angels,
Sing in exultation,
Sing, all ye citizens of heaven above,
Glory to God in the highest!

CHORUS

3. Yea, Lord, we greet Thee,
Born this happy morning;
Jesus, to Thee be glory given,
Word of the Father,
Now in flesh appearing.

CHORUS

IN THE BLEAK MID-WINTER

1. In the bleak mid-winter,
Frosty wind made moan,
Earth stood hard as iron,
Water like a stone;
Snow had fallen, snow on snow,
Snow on snow,
In the bleak mid-winter
Long ago.

2. Our God, heaven cannot hold him
Nor earth sustain;
Heaven and earth shall flee away
When he comes to reign
In the bleak mid-winter
A stable-place sufficed
The Lord God Almighty
Jesus Christ

3. Angels and archangels
May have gathered there,
Cherubim and seraphim
Thronged the air,
But his mother only,
In her maiden bliss,
Worshipped the Beloved
With a kiss.

4. What can I give Him,
Poor as I am?
If I were a shepherd,
I would bring a lamb;
If I were a wise man,
I would do my part;
Yet what I can I give Him,
Give my heart.

Christina Georgina Rossetti, 1830-94

HARK THE HERALD ANGELS SING

1   Hark! the herald-angels sing
Glory to the new-born King,
Peace on earth, and mercy mild,
God and sinners reconciled.
Joyful, all ye nations, rise,
Join the triumph of the skies:
With the angelic host proclaim
Christ is born in Bethlehem.

CHORUS
Hark! the herald-angels sing
Glory to the new-born King.

2 Christ, by highest heaven adored.
Christ, the everlasting Lord,
Late in time behold Him come,
Offspring of a virgin's womb!
Veiled in flesh the Godhead see;
Hail the incarnate Deity!
Pleased as man with men to dwell,
Jesus, our Immanuel.

CHORUS

3   Mild He lays His glory by,
Born that man no more may die,
Born to raise the sons of earth.
Born to give them second birth.
Hail the heaven-born Prince of Peace!
Hail the Sun of Righteousness!
Light and life to all he brings,
Risen with healing in His wings.

CHORUS

Charles Wesley, 1707 - 88

WHILE SHEPHERDS WATCHED THEIR FLOCKS BY NIGHT

1 While shepherds watched their flocks by night,
All seated on the ground,
The angel of the Lord came down
And glory shone around.

2   Fear not! said he: for mighty dread
Had seized their troubled mind
Glad tidings of great joy I bring
To you and all mankind.

3   To you, in David's town, this day
Is born, of David's line,
A Saviour, who is Christ the Lord;
And this shall be the sign.

4   The heavenly Babe you there shall find
To human view displayed,
All meanly wrapped in swaddling bands
And in a manger laid.

5   Thus spake the seraph; and forthwith
Appeared a shining throng
Of angels praising God, and thus
Addressed their joyful song.

6   All glory be to God on High,
And to the earth be peace;
Good will henceforth from heaven to man
Begin and never cease! Amen.

Nahum Tate, 1652 - 1715

WHILE SHEPHERDS WATCHED THEIR FLOCKS BY NIGHT

1 While shepherds watched their flocks by night
All seated on the ground,
The angel of the Lord came down
And glory shone around.

2 Fear not said he; for mighty dread
Had seized their troubled mind
Glad tidings of great joy I bring
To you and all mankind.

3 To you, in David's town, this day
Is born, of David's line,
A Saviour, who is Christ the Lord,
And this shall be the sign.

4 The heavenly Babe you there shall find
To human view displayed,
All meanly wrapped in swaddling bands,
And in a manger laid.

5 Thus spake the seraph, and forthwith
Appeared a shining throng,
Of angels praising God, and thus
Addressed their joyful song.

6 All glory be to God on High,
And to the earth be peace;
Good will henceforth from heaven to men
Begin and never cease! Amen.

Nahum Tate 1652 - 1715

HARK THE HERALD ANGELS SING

1 Hark the herald-angels sing
Glory to the new-born King,
Peace on earth, and mercy mild,
God and sinners reconciled.
Joyful, all ye nations, rise,
Join the triumph of the skies,
With the angelic host proclaim
Christ is born in Bethlehem.

CHORUS
Hark the herald-angels sing,
Glory to the new-born King.

2 Christ, by highest heaven adored,
Christ, the everlasting Lord,
Late in time behold Him come,
Offspring of a virgin's womb.
Veiled in flesh the Godhead see,
Hail the incarnate Deity!
Pleased as man with men to dwell,
Jesus, our Emmanuel.

CHORUS

3 Mild He lays His glory by,
Born that man no more may die,
Born to raise the sons of earth,
Born to give them second birth.
Hail the heaven born Prince of Peace!
Hail the Sun of Righteousness!
Light and life to all He brings,
Risen with healing in His wings.

CHORUS

Charles Wesley, 1707 - 88

O LITTLE TOWN OF BETHLEHEM

1   O little town of Bethlehem,
    How still we see thee lie!
    Above thy deep and dreamless sleep
    The silent stars go by:
    Yet in they dark street shineth
    The everlasting Light:
    The hopes and fears of all the years
    Are met in thee to-night.

2   O morning stars, together
    Proclaim the holy birth,
    And praises sing to God the King,
    And peace to men one earth;
    For Chrst is born of Mary;
    And, gathered all above,
    While mortals sleep, the angels keep
    Their watch of wondering love.

3   How silently, how silently
    The wondrous gift is given!
    So God imparts to human hearts
    The blessings of His heaven.
    No ear may hear His coming;
    But in this world of sin,
    Where the meek souls will receive Him, still
    The dear Christ enters in.

4   O holy child of Bethlehem,
    Descend to us, we pray;
    Cast out our sin, and enter in;
    Be born in us to-day.
    We hear the Christmas angels
    The great glad tidings tell;
    O come to us abide with us
    Our Lord Emmanuel.   Amen.

Philip Brooks, 1835 - 93

WE THREE KINGS OF ORIENT ARE

1   We three kings of Orient are;
    Bearing gifts we traverse afar
    Field and fountain, moor and mountain,
    Following yonder star:

    CHORUS
    O star of wonder, star of night,
    Star with royal beauty bright,
    Westward leading, still proceeding,
    Guide us to Thy perfect light.

2   Born a king on Bethlehem plain,
    Gold I bring, to crown him again -
    King for ever, ceasing never,
    Over us all to reign:

    CHORUS

3   Frankincense to offer have I;
    Incense owns a Deity nigh;
    Prayer and praising all men raising,
    Worship Him, God most high:

    CHORUS

4   Myrrh is mine; its bitter perfume
    Breathes a life of gathering gloom;
    Sorrowing, sighing, bleeding, dying,
    Sealed in the stone-cold tomb:

    CHORUS

5   Glorious now, behold Him arise,
    King and God, and sacrifice!
    Heaven sings 'Alleluia',
    'Alleluia' the earth replies:

    CHORUS

John Henry Hopkins Junr., 1820 - 91

THE TWELVE DAYS OF CHRISTMAS

Use the drawings on page 38 to illustrate this carol,

On the first day of Christmas
My true love sent to me -
A partridge in a pear tree.

On the second day of Christmas
My true love sent to me -
Two turtle doves
And a partridge in a pear tree.

On the third day of Christmas
My true love sent to me -
Three French hens,
Two turtle doves

. . .

On the fourth day of Christmas
My true love sent to me -
Four calling birds,
Three French hens,

. . .

On the fifth day of Christmas
My true love sent to me -
Five golden rings,
Four calling birds,

. . .

On the sixth day of Christmas
My true love sent to me -
Six geese a-laying,
Five golden rings,

. . .

On the seventh day of Christmas
My true love sent to me -
Seven swans a-swimming,
Six geese a-laying,

. . .

THE TWELVE DAYS OF CHRISTMAS

Use the drawings on page 38 to illustrate this carol.

On the first day of Christmas
My true love sent to me -
A partridge in a pear tree.

On the second day of Christmas
My true love sent to me
Two turtle doves
And a partridge in a pear tree.

On the third day of Christmas
My true love sent to me
Three French hens
Two turtle doves.

On the fourth day of Christmas
My true love sent to me
Four calling birds,
Three French hens.

On the fifth day of Christmas
My true love sent to me -
Five golden rings,
Four calling birds.

On the sixth day of Christmas
My true love sent to me
Six geese a-laying,
Five golden rings.

On the seventh day of Christmas
My true love sent to me
Seven swans a-swimming,
Six geese a-laying.

On the eighth day of Christmas
My true love sent to me -
Eight maids a-milking,
Seven swans a-swimming,

. . .

On the ninth day of Christmas
My true love sent to me -
Nine drummers drumming,
Eight maids a-milking,

. . .

On the tenth day of Christmas
My true love sent to me -
Ten pipers piping,
Nine drummers drumming,

. . .

On the eleventh day of Christmas
My true love sent to me -
Eleven dames a-dancing,
Ten pipers piping,

. . .

On the twelfth day of Christmas
My true love sent to me -
Twelve lords a-leaping,
Eleven dames a-dancing,

. . .

YULETIDE

The tradition of the twelve days of Christmas goes back to the pagan Yuletide feast of northern Europe. This was held at the time of the winter solstice and lasted for 12 days. In prehistoric days to help the 'dying' sun, people lit bonfires to give it light and warmth.

The custom of carrying Yule logs into Norsemen's houses goes back to the Middle Ages. A huge log chosen from a forest tree, was dragged home and decorated with greenery and ribbons. After it had dried, it was burned over the 12 days of Yuletide. Nordic people believed that this had a magical effect and helped the sun to shine brightly. Some of the log was kept because it was also thought to keep away evil spirits. The following year it was used to kindle the new log.

On the eighth day of Christmas
My true love sent to me -
Eight maids a-milking,
Seven swans a-swimming,

On the ninth day of Christmas
My true love sent to me -
Nine drummers drumming,
Eight maids a-milking,

On the tenth day of Christmas
My true love sent to me -
Ten pipers piping,
Nine drummers drumming,

On the eleventh day of Christmas
My true love sent to me -
Eleven dancers a-dancing,
Ten pipers piping,

On the twelfth day of Christmas
My true love sent to me -
Twelve lords a-leaping,
Eleven dancers a-dancing,

YULETIDE

The tradition of the twelve days of Christmas goes back to the pagan Yuletide feast of northern Europe. This was held at the time of the winter solstice and lasted for 12 days. In prehistoric days to help the dying sun, people lit bonfires to give it light and warmth.

The custom of carrying Yule logs into Norsemen's houses goes back to the Middle Ages. A huge log chosen from a forest tree, was dragged home and decorated with greenery and ribbons. After it had dried, it was burned over the 12 days of Yuletide. Nordic people believed that this had a magical effect and helped the sun to shine brightly. Some of the log was kept, because it was also thought to keep away evil spirits. The following year it was used to kindle the new log.

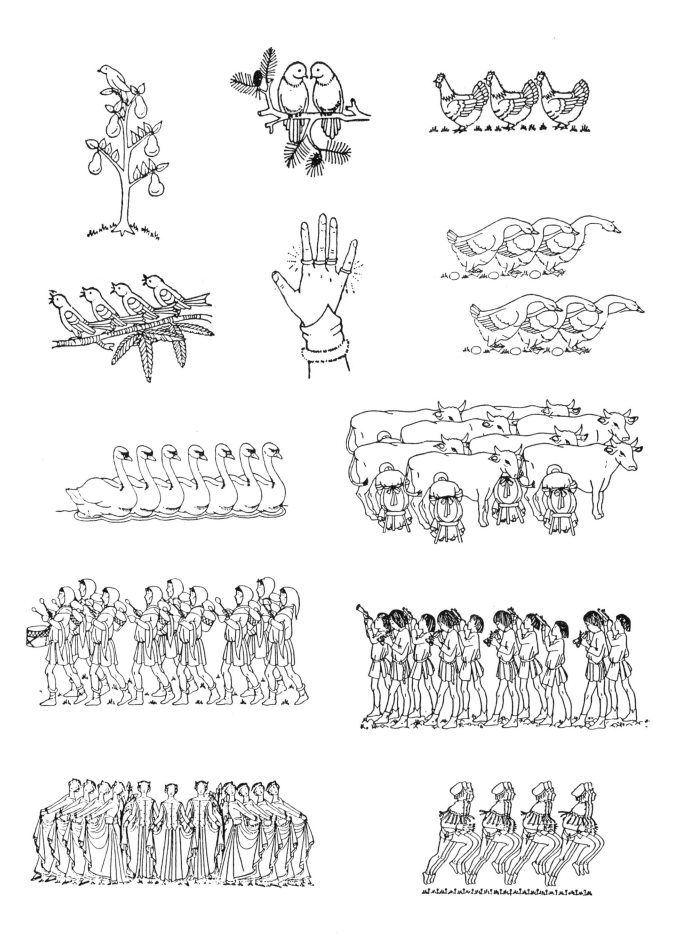

Use these pictures to illustrate the carol, THE TWELVE DAYS OF CHRISTMAS

CHRISTMAS FACTS

CHRISTMAS DAY In 354, Pope Gregory proclaimed December 25 as the date of the Nativity, the date on which the birth of Christ should be celebrated. In 1552 the English Puritans banned Christmas. Although Christmas returned to England with Charles II in 1660, it did not become really popular until Victorian times.

THE NATIVITY AND THE CHRISTMAS CRIB In 1224, St. Francis of Assisi asked the Pope's permission to recreate the nativity scene as part of the celebrations of Christmas. Cribs became popular in the UK in the middle of the 19th. century, mainly in Roman Catholic churches. They are found in most churches now.

THE CHRISTMAS TREE The custom of decorating a tree at Christmas started in Germany. St. Boniface, the English missionary to Germany in the 8th. century is said to have set up a fir tree hung with offerings to the Christ-child in place of the oak that was sacred to the pagan god Thor. By the 16th. century, fir trees decorated with apples, sweets and paper roses were to be found in many German homes. Later, candles and glittering decorations were added to what became known as the Christmas tree. The custom spread to Britain but it was Prince Albert, husband of Queen Victoria, who helped to make it popular here. In 1841 the Prince had a tree from his native Germany set up in Windsor castle for the royal family.

CHRISTMAS CARDS The first Christmas card was produced in 1846. The custom of sending cards became popular when the halfpenny post was introduced in 1870 for cards sent in an unsealed envelope. By 1880, the Post Office was asking every one 'to post early for Christmas'.

CHRISTMAS WREATHS Evergreens have been used to decorate the home since early times. The Victorians made 'welcome' wreaths of holly, ivy, pine cones and ribbons and hung them on the front door.

HOLLY Today holly is associated with Christ's crucifixion. The sharp leaves represent the crown of thorns and the red berries drops of His blood.

FATHER CHRISTMAS was a Christian bishop called Nicholas who lived in the 3rd. or 4th. century. He is said to have dropped bars of gold through the windows of a starving family. Legend says this is how the custom of secretly giving presents to children on Christmas Day started. Santa Claus, another name for Father Christmas, comes from Sant Nikolaas, the Dutch for St. Nicholas.

CHRISTMAS CRACKERS These were invented by a young baker, Tom Smith, who saw sweets wrapped in coloured paper in France. He made similar sweets in England and when the sale of these dropped, he included a piece of chemically treated paper which went 'bang' when the cracker was pulled and broken. This novelty caught on and by 1900 he was selling 13 million crackers all over the world.

BOXING DAY The name comes from the 'dole of the Christmas Box', a custom from the Middle Ages when alms boxes were placed in churches at Christmas to collect money. These were opened on the day after Christmas and the money given to the poor of the parish. Today, as a way of saying thank you, it is usual to give 'Christmas boxes' to people who have served the community well throughout the year.

TWELFTH NIGHT, January 6, the day before Epiphany, the feast celebrating the visit of the Three Kings to the Christ-child in Bethlehem. It is the day on which Christmas cards and decorations are taken down. Once a special cake, Twelfth Night Cake was baked but this has been replaced by the traditional Christmas cake.

CHRISTMAS CUSTOMS AROUND THE WORLD

In **Britain,** Father Christmas is pictured in a red cloak and hood in a sledge drawn by reindeer and children hang up their Christmas stockings for him to fill with presents.

In Switzerland and Germany, Father Christmas is always shown wearing bishop's robes.

In **Swiss** villages there is a procession round the village - first comes a watchman blowing a bugle, then two 'demons' and a man disguised as a goat. Santa's servant has a sack into which he threatens to put any naughty children. Lastly, there is Santa Claus who banishes the demons and goat and distributes gifts.

In the **Netherlands and Belgium** on December 6, the night before St. Nicholas' day, children leave their wooden shoes filled with hay for the white horse that Santa Claus rides.

France French children believe it is the Christ-child who brings gifts and they put their shoes in the hearth on Christmas Eve.

In **Italy,** some people eat very little during Christmas Day, spending the time in prayer. They often have beautiful cribs in their homes and churches. Italians give presents to each other on January 6th. when the wise men brought their gifts to Jesus. The gifts are supposed to have come down the chimney, brought by a woman on a broomstick.

In **Poland,** Christmas Eve is called the Festival of the Star. Sometimes Polish people do not eat until the first star appears in the sky and a place is always left at the table for the Christ-child. Young boys in the family may dress up as the wise men and distribute presents.

Sweden On Christmas Eve there are parties and presents. Christmas food often includes cooked cod fish and rice porridge.

In **Australia and New Zealand** where December is hot and sunny, houses are decorated with flowers and celebrations are often held out of doors. Christmas dinner is often eaten as a picnic on the beach and Santa may arrive by surfboat instead of a sleigh.

In **Mexico,** each night from 16th. December, groups of people carrying candles and following statues of Joseph and Mary go from door to door and ask to be 'allowed in' as Mary and Joseph did on the first Christmas night. The 'innkeepers' turn them away until they arrive at a house where there is a party. Usually there is also a home-made crib. It is a Christmas tradition to set out luminarias, special lights, along the path to the house. The lights are believed to light the way for Mary, Joseph and the baby.

Ask your friends how they celebrate Christmas.

CHRISTMAS CUSTOMS
AROUND THE WORLD

In Britain, Father Christmas is pictured in a red cloak and hood in a sledge drawn by reindeer and children hang up their Christmas stockings for him to fill with presents.

In Switzerland and Germany, Father Christmas is always shown wearing bishop's robes.

In Swiss villages there is a procession round the village - first comes a watchman blowing a bugle, then two demons and a man disguised as a goat. Santa's servant has a sack into which he threatens to put any naughty children. Lastly, there is Santa Claus who banishes the demons and goat and distributes gifts.

In the Netherlands and Belgium on December 6, the night before St. Nicholas' day, children leave their wooden shoes filled with hay for the white horse that Santa Claus rides.

In France, French children believe it is the Christ-child who brings gifts and they put their shoes in the hearth on Christmas Eve.

In Italy, some families start very little on Christmas Day, spending the time in prayer. They often have candles lit in their homes and churches. Italians give presents to each other on January 6th, when the wise men brought their gifts to Jesus. The gifts are supposed to have come down the chimney, brought by a woman on a broomstick.

In Poland, Christmas Eve is called the Festival of the Star. Sometimes Polish people do not eat until the first star appears in the sky and a place is always left at the table for the Christ-child. Young boys in the family may dress up as the wise men and distribute presents.

In Sweden On Christmas Eve there are parties and presents. Christmas food often includes cooked cod fish and rice porridge.

In Australia and New Zealand where December is hot and sunny, houses are decorated with flowers and celebrations are often held out of doors. Christmas dinner is often eaten as a picnic on the beach and Santa may arrive by surfboat instead of a sleigh.

In Mexico, each night from 16th December, groups of people carrying candles and following statues of Joseph and Mary go from door to door and ask to be 'allowed in' as Mary and Joseph did on the first Christmas night. The 'makeeepers' turn them away until they arrive at a house where there is a party. Usually there is also a home-made crib. It is a Christmas tradition to set out luminaries, special lights, along the path to the house. The lights are believed to light the way for Mary, Joseph and the baby.

Ask your friends how they celebrate Christmas.

These drawings are about Christmas. To which country does each belong?

*Peace and Joy
at Christmas*

Bethlehem

*Peace and Goodwill
at Christmas*

Colour these pictures to make Christmas cards. Choose a greeting from page 45
or write your own verse.

Peace and Joy at Christmas

Peace and Goodwill at Christmas

Colour these pictures to make Christmas cards. Choose a greeting from page 45 or write your own verse.

Season's Greetings

Merry Christmas

Colour these pictures to make Christmas cards. Choose a greeting from page 45 or write your own verse.

Season's
Greetings

Merry Christmas

Colour these pictures to make Christmas cards. Choose a greeting from page 45 or write your own verse.

You have a friend living abroad. Design this Christmas card so that it tells him or her what Christmas is like in this country. Choose a greeting from page 45 or write your own verse.

Write a letter to your friend describing how you will spend Christmas. Include what you do in school just before the end of the term and during the Christmas holiday.

[Reminders:
Decorate the school and tree
Special Christmas service at school
School plays
Carol singing
School Christmas post
School party
Other parties
Help for others in the community
Decorate tree at home

Shopping
Wrapping presents
Visiting relatives and friends
Christmas religious services
Waiting for Santa
Christmas Day
Visitors
Food
Special tasks you had to carry out.]

You have a friend living abroad. Design this Christmas card so that it tells him or her what Christmas is like in this country. Choose a greeting from page 45 or write your own verse.

Write a letter to your friend describing how you will spend Christmas. Include what you do in school just before the end of the term and during the Christmas holiday.

[Reminders:

Decorate the school and tree	Shopping
Special Christmas service at school	Wrapping presents
School plays	Visiting relatives and friends
Carol singing	Christmas religious services
School Christmas post	Waiting for Santa
School party	Christmas Day
Other parties	Visitors
Help for others in the community	Food
Decorate tree at home	Special tasks you had to carry out]

*Merry Christmas and
Best Wishes for the
New Year*

*Best Wishes
for Christmas
and the New Year*

**HAPPY
CHRISTMAS**

***Merry Christmas and
Best Wishes for the
New Year***

***Best Wishes
for Christmas
and the New Year***

***HAPPY
CHRISTMAS***

With all Good Wishes
for
Christmas and the New Year

*Wishing you Joy and Peace
for Christmas
and throughout the New Year*

*Wishing you
a Merry Christmas
and every happiness
in the New Year*

Season's Greetings

***To Mum**
Lots of Love*

***Peace and Goodwill
at Christmas
and throughout
the New Year***

***To Dad**
Lots of Love*

***To Mum and Dad
Lots of Love
at Christmas
From***

HAPPY
CHRISTMAS

Best Wishes
for Christmas
and the New Year

Merry Christmas and
Best Wishes for the
New Year

HAPPY
CHRISTMAS

Best Wishes
for Christmas
and the New Year

Merry Christmas and
Best Wishes for the
New Year

Wishing you Joy and Peace
for Christmas
and throughout the New Year

With all Good Wishes
for
Christmas and the New Year

Wishing you
a Merry Christmas
and every happiness
in the New Year

Season's Greetings

Peace and Goodwill
at Christmas
and throughout
the New Year

To Mum
Lots of Love

To Mum and Dad
Lots of Love
at Christmas
From

To Dad
Lots of Love

THE CHRISTMAS POST

Sending and receiving cards is an exciting part of Christmas. Once letters had to be carried by messengers on horseback or by horse drawn coaches. Usually, the journey had to be done in stages with stops at roadside inns. Sending a letter was expensive and slow.

Today, the mail travels overnight in long trains. A letter or card posted one day may be delivered anywhere in the UK within twenty four hours. Letters to overseas countries travel quickly by aeroplane or more slowly by ship. Airmail from the UK reaches Canada and the USA within two days and Australia and New Zealand in under a week. Postage stamps were introduced in 1840. Before that the person receiving the letter had to pay the cost of postage. Christmas cards usually cost less to post than other mail.

The postman collects the mail from post office boxes and post offices. This is taken to the sorting office. Here machines detect special lines on the stamps. The machines turn the letters so that they all face the same way and cancel the stamps. The letters are then sorted according to their post codes - the letters and numbers at the end of the addresses. Finally, they end up in the postman's mail bag to be delivered through someone's letter box.

Find out the last date for the Christmas post for different places.

How much does it cost to post a Christmas card?

What is your post code?

Why do you think it is quicker to sort letters according to their post codes instead of their full addresses?

THE CHRISTMAS POST

Sending and receiving cards is an exciting part of Christmas. Once letters had to be carried by messengers on horseback, or by horse-drawn coaches. Usually, the journey had to be done in stages with stops at roadside inns. Sending a letter was expensive and slow.

Today, the mail travels overnight in long trains. A letter or card posted one day may be delivered anywhere in the UK within twenty-four hours. Letters to overseas countries travel quickly by aeroplane or more slowly by ship. Airmail from the UK reaches Canada and the USA within two days and Australia and New Zealand in under a week. Postage stamps were introduced in 1840. Before that the person receiving the letter had to pay the cost of postage. Christmas cards usually cost less to post than other mail.

The postman collects the mail from post office boxes and post offices. This is taken to the sorting office. Here, machines detect special lines on the stamps. The machines turn the letters so that they all face the same way, and cancel the stamps. The letters are then sorted according to their post codes – the letters and numbers at the end of the addresses. Finally, they end up in the postman's mail bag, to be delivered through someone's letter box.

Find out the last date for the Christmas post for different places.

How much does it cost to post a Christmas card?

What is your post code?

Why do you think it is quicker to sort letters according to their postcodes instead of their full addresses?

Christmas Past...

CHRISTMAS
POST

CHRISTMAS POST

These are Christmas stamps for the school Christmas post.

Collect used stamps from overseas countries.

What is a stamp collector called?

Where is a stamp stuck on an envelope?

What shape are 'real stamps'? Why is this shape used?

Why are 'real stamps' usually quite small?

Design and draw a Christmas stamp.

These are Christmas stamps for the school Christmas post.

Collect used stamps from oversects countries.

What is a stamp collector called?

Where is a stamp stuck on an envelope?

What shape are real stamps? Why is this shape used?

Why are real stamps usually quite small?

Design and draw a Christmas stamp.

To
From

Merry Christmas

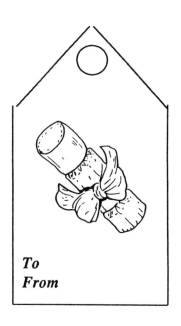

To
From

To
From

Merry Christmas

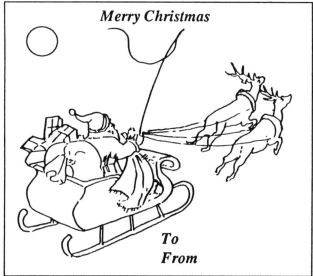

To
From

To
From

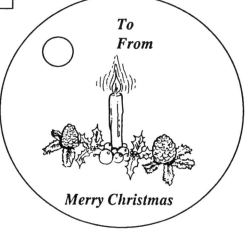

To
From

Merry Christmas

Using a Christmas gift tag is a good way of saying who a present is for and who is sending it.

Design your own gift tags.

TINY TIM

'And how did little Tim behave?' asked Mrs Cratchit.

'As good as gold,' said Bob, 'and better. Somehow he gets thoughtful sitting by himself so much, and thinks the strangest things you ever heard. He told me, coming home, that he hoped the people saw him in the church, because he was a cripple, and it might be pleasant to them to remember upon Christmas Day, who made lame beggars walk, and blind men see.'

Bob's voice was shaking when he told them this, and trembled more when he said that Tiny Tim was growing strong and hearty.

His active little crutch was heard upon the floor, and back came Tiny Tim before another word was spoken, escorted by his brother and sister to his stool before the fire; and while Bob, turning up his cuffs - as if, poor fellow, they were capable of being made more shabby - made some hot mixture in a jug with gin and lemons, and stirred it round and round and put it on the hob to simmer; Master Peter, and the two young Cratchits went to fetch the goose, with which they soon returned.

There never was such a goose. Bob said he didn't believe there ever was such a goose cooked. Its tenderness and flavour, size and cheapness, were the themes of universal admiration. Eked out by apple sauce and mashed potatoes, it was a sufficient dinner for the whole family; indeed, as Mrs Crachit said with great delight (surveying one small atom of bone upon the dish), they hadn't eaten it all. Yet every one had had enough, and the youngest Cratchits in particular, were steeped in sage and onion to the eyebrows! But now, the plates being changed by Miss Belinda, Mrs. Cratchit left the room alone - too nervous to bear witnesses - to take the pudding out and bring it in.

'Oh a wonderful pudding!' Bob Cratchit said, and calmly too, that he regarded it as the greatest success achieved by Mrs. Cratchit since their marriage. Mrs. Cratchit said that now the weight was off her mind, she would confess she had had her doubts about the quantity of flour. Everybody had something to say about it, but nobody said it was a small pudding for a large family.

At last dinner was all over, the cloth was cleared, the hearth swept, and the fire made up. The mixture in the jug being tasted and considered perfect, the apples and oranges were put upon the table, and a shovelful of chestnuts on the fire. Then all the Cratchit family sat round the hearth, in what Bob Cratchit called a circle, and at Bob Cratchit's elbow stood the family display of glass, two tumblers and a large pot without a handle.

These held the hot stuff from the jug, however, as well as golden goblets would have done; and Bob served it out with beaming looks, while the chestnuts on the fire sputtered and cracked noisily. Then Bob proposed:

'A Merry Christmas to us all, my dears. God bless us!'

Which all the family re-echoed.

'God bless us every one!' said Tiny Tim, the last of all.

He sat very close to his father's side upon his little stool. Bob held his withered little hand

TINY TIM

"And how did little Tim behave?" asked Mrs Cratchit.

"As good as gold," said Bob, "and better. Somehow he gets thoughtful sitting by himself so much, and thinks the strangest things you ever heard. He told me, coming home, that he hoped the people saw him in the church, because he was a cripple, and it might be pleasant to them to remember upon Christmas Day, who made lame beggars walk, and blind men see."

Bob's voice was shaking when he told them this, and trembled more when he said that Tim was growing strong and hearty.

His active little crutch was heard upon the floor, and back came Tiny Tim before another word was spoken, escorted by his brother and sister to his stool before the fire; and while Bob, turning up his cuffs - as if, poor fellow, they were capable of being made more shabby - made some hot mixture in a jug with gin and lemons, and stirred it round and round and put it on the hob to simmer; Master Peter, and the two young Cratchits went to fetch the goose, with which they soon returned.

There never was such a goose. Bob said he didn't believe there ever was such a goose cooked. Its tenderness and flavour, size and cheapness, were the themes of universal admiration. Eked out by apple-sauce and mashed potatoes, it was a sufficient dinner for the whole family; indeed, as Mrs Cratchit said with great delight (surveying one small atom of bone upon the dish), they hadn't eaten it all! Yet every one had had enough, and the youngest Cratchits in particular, were steeped in sage and onion to the eyebrows! But now, the plates being changed by Miss Belinda, Mrs Cratchit left the room alone - too nervous to bear witnesses - to take the pudding up and bring it in.

"Oh, a wonderful pudding!" Bob Cratchit said, and calmly too, that he regarded it as the greatest success achieved by Mrs Cratchit since their marriage. Mrs Cratchit said that now the weight was off her mind, she would confess she had her doubts about the quantity of flour. Everybody had something to say about it, but nobody said it was, a small pudding for a large family.

At last the dinner was all over, the cloth was cleared, the hearth swept, and the fire made up. The mixture in the jug being tasted and considered perfect, the apples and oranges were put upon the table, and a shovelful of chestnuts on the fire. Then all the Cratchit family sat round the hearth, in what Bob Cratchit called a circle, and at Bob Cratchit's elbow stood the family display of glass. Two tumblers, and a large jug without a handle.

These held the hot stuff from the jug, however, as well as golden goblets would have done; and Bob served it out with beaming looks, while the chestnuts on the fire spluttered and cracked noisily. Then Bob proposed:

"A Merry Christmas to us all, my dears. God bless us!"

Which all the family re-echoed.

"God bless us every one!" said Tiny Tim, the last of all.

He sat very close to his father's side upon his little stool. Bob held his withered little hand in his, as he loved the child, and wished to keep him by his side, and dreaded that he might be taken from him.

[Scrooge and the Ghost of Christmas Present watching the family could not be seen nor heard by the Cratchits.

'Spirit,' said Scrooge, with an interest he had never felt before, 'tell me if Tiny Tim will live.'

'I see a vacant seat,' replied the Ghost, 'in the chimney-corner, and a crutch without an owner, carefully preserved. If these shadows remain unaltered by the Future, the child will die.']

From *A Christmas Carol* by Charles Dickens

Draw and colour a picture of the Cratchits having Christmas dinner or sitting around the hearth.

Were the Cratchits poor or wealthy? How do you know?

What kind of person is called a 'Scrooge'?

Read *A Christmas Carol* and find out why Scrooge is watching the family and what happens to Tiny Tim.

in his, as he loved the child, and wished to keep him by his side, and dreaded that he might be taken from him.

Scrooge and the Ghost of Christmas Present watching the family could not be seen nor heard by the Cratchits.

'Spirit,' said Scrooge, with an interest he had never felt before, 'tell me if Tiny Tim will live.'

'I see a vacant seat,' replied the Ghost, 'in the chimney-corner, and a crutch without an owner, carefully preserved. If these shadows remain unaltered by the Future, the child will die.'

From A Christmas Carol by Charles Dickens

Draw and colour a picture of the Cratchits having Christmas dinner or sitting around the hearth.

Were the Cratchits poor or wealthy? How do you know?

What kind of person is called a Scrooge?

Read A Christmas Carol and find out why Scrooge is watching the family and what happens to Tiny Tim.

FESTIVALS

ADVENT
The twenty eight days leading up to Christmas and the celebration of the birth of Christ. Advent Sunday is the first of the four Sundays of Advent and the one that falls closest to November 30th.

CHRISTMAS AND EPIPHANY
The birth of Christ is celebrated on December, 25 and twelve days later (January 6th.) is Epiphany, the time of the coming of the wise men from the East bringing their gifts to baby Jesus.

THE NEW YEAR
A long time ago, the Egyptians, Phoenicians and Persians began the year on September 21 when day and night have the same length. For a time the Greeks celebrated the beginning of the year on December 21, the shortest day of the year. The Romans did the same until Caesar changed it to January 1. It is traditional to hold parties on December 31, New Year's Eve and 'to see the New Year in with friends'. Church bells ring at midnight. This is a time to remember the past year, sad and happy times, and to make new year resolutions, that is to decide how to be a better person. In Scotland, New Year's Eve is called Hogmanay and there are many parties. By Hogmanay tradition, it is lucky if a dark haired person comes into the house at midnight. This is called first footing.

LENT
A period of six weeks leading up to Easter. It ends with Holy Week. During this time, Christians 'give up' something that they like to do or eat as a mark of remembrance.

PALM SUNDAY
This commemorates the day Jesus entered Jerusalem and was welcomed by the people.

GOOD FRIDAY
This commemorates the crucifixion of Christ.

EASTER SUNDAY
This commemorates the day when some of His friends found His tomb empty and learned that He had risen from the dead.

ASCENSION DAY
Forty days after Easter Sunday when Christ went back to Heaven after telling His disciples how they were to carry on with His work.

WHIT SUNDAY
The day on which God the Holy Spirit visited the disciples.

What New Year Resolutions do you want to make? Do you think you can keep them?

Write a story with pictures about an adventure that begins on New Year's Eve.

FESTIVALS

ADVENT
The twelve eight days leading up to Christmas and the celebration of the birth of Christ. Advent Sunday is the first of the four Sundays of Advent and the one that falls closest to November 30th.

CHRISTMAS AND EPIPHANY
The birth of Christ is celebrated on December 25 and twelve days later (January 6th) is Epiphany, the time of the coming of the wise men from the East bringing their gifts to baby Jesus.

THE NEW YEAR
A long time ago, the Egyptians, Phoenicians and Persians began the year on September 21 when day and night have the same length. From time the Greeks celebrated the beginning of the year on December 21, the shortest day of the year. The Romans did the same until Caesar changed it to January 1st set about to hold parties on December 31, New Year's Eve and to see the New Year in with friends. Church bells ring at midnight. This is a time to remember the past year, and happy times, and to make new year resolutions, that is to decide how to be a better person. In Scotland, New Year's Eve is called Hogmanay and there are many parties. By tradition, it is lucky if a dark haired person comes into the house at midnight. This is called first footing.

LENT
A period of six weeks leading up to Easter. It ends with Holy Week. During this time, Christians give up something that they like to do or eat as a mark of remembrance.

PALM SUNDAY
This commemorates the day Jesus entered Jerusalem and was welcomed by the people.

GOOD FRIDAY
This commemorates the crucifixion of Christ.

EASTER SUNDAY
This commemorates the day when some of His friends found His tomb empty and learned that He had risen from the dead.

ASCENSION DAY
Forty days after Easter Sunday when Christ went back to Heaven after telling His disciples how they were to carry on with His work.

WHIT SUNDAY
The day on which God the Holy Spirit visited the disciples.

What New Year Resolutions do you want to make? Do you think you can keep them?

Write a story with pictures about an adventure that begins on New Year's Eve.

OTHER RELIGIOUS FESTIVALS

Muslim dates do not follow the solar year. They are not fixed and move forward each year.

January or February	**CHINESE NEW YEAR** Chinese make sure that the New Year starts with as much good luck as possible. There are many traditional stories about the twelve animal signs.
*February March	**RAMADAN AND EID UL FITR** This is the period when Muslims fast and subsequently celebrate being a Muslim and living in 'Islam' - that is submission to Allah.
March and April	**PESAKH (Passover)** The Jewish celebration of God freeing the Israelites from slavery in Egypt.
March and April	**HOLI** The festival of love and of the harvest. This celebration recalls the tricks that the god Krishna played.
April 13 Sometimes April 14	**BAISAKHI** The Sikh festival that celebrates the founding of the Khalsa. It says that it is important to stand up for one's beliefs and to defend the helpless.
*May	**EID UL ADHA** The Muslim festival recalling the obedience of Ibrahim and his son Ishmael to the Will of God.
May or June	**WESAK** Buddhists celebrate the three great events in the life of the Buddha: his birth, his enlightenment and his death. These all happened on the same day in different years.
September or October	**YOM KIPPUR AND ROSH HASHANAH** Rosh Hashanah is the Jewish New Year. Yom Kippur, nine days later, is a time for remembering the failures and faults of the past year and preparing for a new start.
October or November	**DIVALI** This celebrates the New Year, and also recalls the story of Rama and Sita from the Ramayana. Oil lamps are burned in the windows of Hindu homes.
November	**GURU NANAK'S BIRTHDAY** The birth of the founder of Sikhism is celebrated by reading the scripture, the Guru Granth Sahib, by singing the hymns he wrote and telling stories about him.

OTHER RELIGIOUS FESTIVALS

*Muslim dates do not follow the solar year. They are not fixed and move forward each year.

January or February	**CHINESE NEW YEAR**	Chinese make sure that the New Year starts with as much good luck as possible. There are many traditional stories about the twelve animal signs.
February March	**RAMADAN AND EID UL-FITR**	This is the period when Muslims fast and subsequently celebrate being a Muslim and living in Islam - that is submission to Allah.
March and April	**PESACH (Passover)**	The Jewish celebration of God freeing the Israelites from slavery in Egypt.
March and April	**HOLI**	The festival of love and of mischievers. His celebration recalls the tricks that the god Krishna played.
April 14	**BAISAKHI**	Sometimes The Sikh festival that celebrates the founding of the Khalsa... it is important to stand up for one's beliefs and to defend the helpless.
May	**EID UL-ADHA**	The Muslim festival recalling the obedience of Ibrahim and his son Ishmael to the will of God.
May or June	**WESAK**	Buddhists celebrate the three great events in the life of the Buddha: his birth, his enlightenment and his death. These all happened on the same day in different years.
September or October	**YOM KIPPUR AND ROSH HASHANAH**	Rosh Hashanah is the Jewish New Year. Yom Kippur, nine days later, is a time for remembering the failings and faults of the past year and preparing for a new start.
October or November	**DIWALI**	This celebrates the New Year, and also recalls the story of Rama and Sita from the Ramayana. Oil lamps are burned in the windows of Hindu homes.
November	**GURU NANAK'S BIRTHDAY**	The birth of the founder of Sikhism is celebrated by reading the scripture, the Guru Granth Sahib, by singing the hymns he wrote and telling stories about him.

AN ADVENT CALENDAR

Advent means *approach* or *coming*. The time containing the four Sundays before Christmas is called Advent. Since the 6th. century, the Christian church has used this time to prepare for Christmas and the celebration of Christ's birth. This time is often represented in special Advent Calendars. It is apt to combine this with giving. If the numbers sheet is stuck on to a strong carrier bag or suitable box and slits cut between the rows of numbers than the children can drop two pence pieces into the box on each day. The money collected can then be donated to a charity or cause.

After pasting the numbers sheet on the carrier bag, cut slits.
Close the bag with staples or sellotape.

AN ADVENT CALENDAR

Advent means approach or coming. The time containing the four Sundays before Christmas is called Advent. Since the 6th century, the Christian church has used this time to prepare for Christmas and the celebration of Christ's birth. This time is often represented in special Advent Calendars. It is apt to combine this with giving. If the numbers sheet is stuck on to a strong carrier bag or suitable box, and slits cut between the rows of numbers than the children can drop two pence pieces into the box on each day. The money collected can then be donated to a charity or cause.

After pasting the numbers sheet on the carrier bag, cut slits.
Close the bag with staples or sellotape.

1	8	15	22
2	9	16	23
3	10	17	24
4	11	18	25
5	12	19	26
6	13	20	27
7	14	21	28

A SEASONAL CALENDAR

The four drawings on page 56 represent the four seasons of the year. Colour each drawing and cut it out. Paste it on a piece of cardboard with the months below. How do you know which months go with each picture? Underneath write the things you like to do at different times of year.

Some suggestions are

A SEASONAL CALENDAR

The four drawings on page 56 represent the four seasons of the year. Colour each drawing and cut it out. Paste it on a piece of cardboard with the months below. How do you know which months go with each picture? Underneath write the things you like to do at different times of year.

Some suggestions are

A SEASONAL CALENDAR

A SEASONAL CALENDAR

DECORATE A CHRISTMAS TREE

Decorate this Christmas tree. Draw a star or fairy at the top, draw 8 baubles and
11 fairy lights (1 orange, 2 blue, 3 yellow and the rest red) on the branches.
Don't forget the presents at the bottom.

MAKE A CHRISTMAS STAR

Paste these stars on to thin card. Cut them out and cover both sides of them with glitter. Put the big one on the top of the tree and hang the others on the branches or make a star mobile.

MAKE AN ANGEL

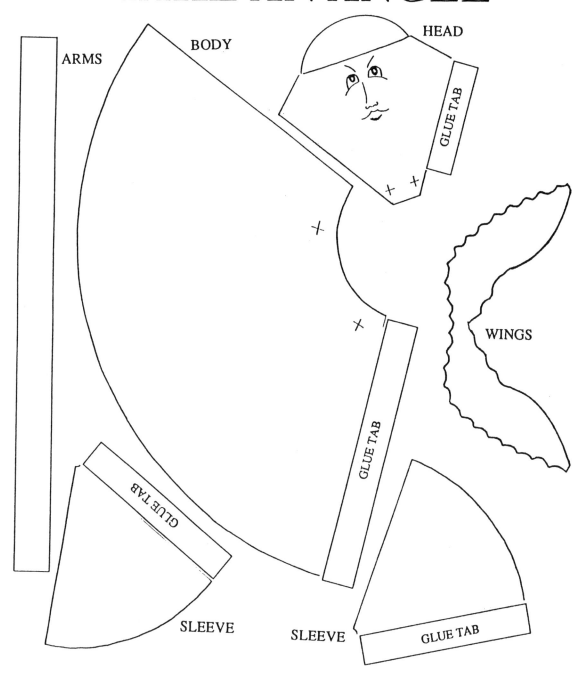

Paste these pieces on to thin card. Cut them out to make an angel for the top of a Christmas tree.

Make holes on the marks +.

Roll the arm piece into a narrow tube.

Pass the tube through a hole in the body piece then through the two holes at the base of the head and out through the other hole in the body piece.

Fold the head piece and glue the tab.

Fold the body piece and glue the tab so that it makes a cone.

Fold each sleeve piece and glue the tab.

Place the sleeves over the arms leaving the ends of the arms sticking out as hands. Fold arms so that the hands rest on the front of the body piece.

Cover the wings with glitter and glue to the back of the angel.

MAKE AN ANGEL

Paste these pieces on to thin card. Cut them out to make an
angel for the top of a Christmas tree.
Make holes on the marks +.
Roll the arm piece into a narrow tube.
Pass the tube through a hole in the body piece then through
the two holes at the base of the head and out through the
other hole in the body piece.
Fold the head piece and glue the tab.
Fold the body piece and glue the tab so that it makes a cone.
Fold each sleeve piece and glue the tab.
Place the sleeves over the arms leaving the ends of the arms sticking out as
hands. Fold arms so that the hands rest on the front of the body piece.
Cover the wings with glitter and glue to the back of the angel.

MAKE SANTA CLAUS

Colour these pieces and paste them on thin card. Cut them out. Pin them together using split pins or thread at the points marked + to make Santa. If you like, glue cotton wool to make his hair and beard.

MAKE SANTA CLAUS

Colour these pieces and paste them on thin card. Cut them out. Pin them together using split pins or thread at the points marked + to make Santa. If you like, glue cotton wool to make his hat and beard.

MAKE A STAINED GLASS WINDOW

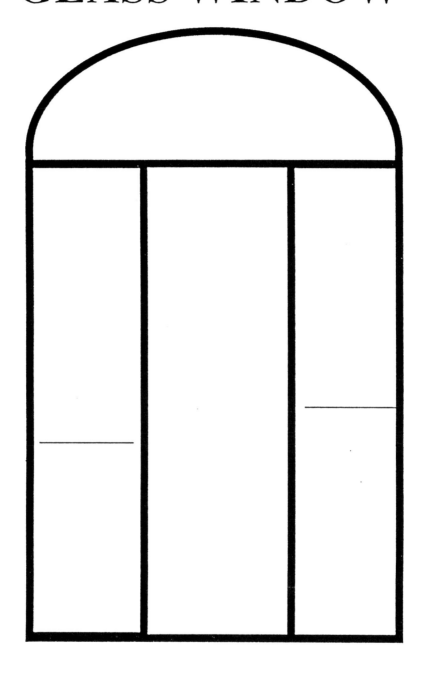

Fill in the paper window with drawings about Christmas. (There are suggestions on page 62.) Colour the pictures you have drawn in the window with felt tipped pens.

Pour a little cooking oil on to a small ball of cotton wool and gently rub the back of the paper window with the oil.

Cut out the paper window and stick on to a glass window so that light can shine through it.

These are some ideas about Christmas for a stained glass window.

You may prefer to choose another theme such as wintertime or your school,

town or village, or children or animals.

THE ROBIN AND THE SNOWMAN

Once two children, Mark and Sally, lived in a house that had a large garden with a river at the bottom.

One night it snowed and when the children woke up everything in the garden was white.

'Let's build a snowman,' said Mark. And they did. They gave him a hat for his head and a red scarf to cheer him up.

When they went to bed they could see the snowman clearly in the moonlight. 'He looks very lonely,' said Sally.

A robin in a tree watching the children make the snowman was so interested that he fell off the branch.

He hurt his wing and could not fly. That night the little bird was cold and frightened. He could not get back to his nest.

The snowman could hear the robin trying to fly and falling back to the ground.

'Can you reach my hat?' he asked. 'You would be warm and safe there until the morning.'

With a great deal of flapping, the robin at last managed to land on the snowman's hat. Quickly he snuggled down inside and fell asleep.

The snowman watched the sun rise and felt sad. He knew that the warmth of the sun would make him melt.

The sun woke the robin too. He felt much better and stretching his wings flew to the top of the tree. 'Thank you Mr Snowman,' he said swooping low.

By mid morning the snowman had melted. Just his hat and scarf remained.

Only you and I know how the snowman helped the robin.

THE ROBIN AND THE SNOWMAN

Once two children, Mark and Sally, lived in a house that had a large garden with a river at the bottom.

One night it snowed and when the children woke up everything in the garden was white.

"Let's build a snowman," said Mark. And they did. They gave him a hat for his head and a red scarf to cheer him up.

When they went to bed they could see the snowman clearly in the moonlight. "He looks very lonely," said Sally.

A robin in a tree watching the children make the snowman was so interested that he fell off the branch.

He hurt his wing and could not fly. That night the little bird was cold and frightened. He could not get back to his nest.

The snowman could hear the robin trying to fly and falling back to the ground.

"Can you reach my hat?" he asked. "You would be warm and safe there until the morning.

With a great deal of flapping, the robin at last managed to land on the snowman's hat. Quickly he snuggled down inside and fell asleep.

The snowman watched the sun rise and felt sad. He knew that the warmth of the sun would make him melt.

The sun woke the robin too. He felt much better and stretching his wings flew to the top of the tree. "Thank you Mr Snowman," he said swooping low.

By mid morning the snowman had melted. Just his hat and scarf remained. Only you and I know how the snowman helped the robin.

The Robin and the Snowman

Colour the robin and the snowman. Draw a scarf on the snowman and colour it red.

In what way was the snowman kind? Why was he sad when he saw the sun rise?

HELPING OTHERS

Make sure that the help offered is the kind that is needed. People in need often find it difficult to accept help but at Christmas people are usually grateful for gifts. Do not take on more than you can do. Remember the most valuable thing you can give is your time. Always respect the privacy and dignity of someone you are visiting.

1. Collect for the elderly and those in need.
> Money to buy Christmas presents (especially food).
> Warm clothing and blankets.
> Tins of food.
> Food including some treats for Christmas hampers.

2. Knit
> squares to make blankets - there is usually a local organisation already doing this - ask at your church or your doctor's surgery. These are easy and really useful at home and overseas.
> Kinit scarves, gloves and hats. Be sure that the colours are 'sensible'.

3.Visit - visits to establishments must always be pre-arranged. Call in to see the person in charge or phone. If it is a group or class visit confirm the arrangements in writing stating the date, time, purpose and how many will be coming. Nothing is so cheering as young faces but adequate supervision is essential.
> Hospital - singing carols and play reading.
> Old People's Homes.
> The elderly in their own homes.
> Relatives.
> Friends.

4. Help generally with
> housework.
> errands.
> cleaning.
> gardening.

5. At home help with
> chores.
> washing up.
> tidying your own room.
> making your own bed.

6. On Christmas Day
> help with the preparation of the Christmas fare.
> help to tidy the house.
> make any visitors feel especially welcome.
> help look after younger brothers and sisters.
> help to clear up toys - people often fall over presents left on the floor.
> help to look after pets.
> be appreciative of all the work that has been done to make Christmas Day special.

HELPING OTHERS

Make sure that the help offered is the kind that is needed. People in need often find it difficult to accept help but at Christmas people are usually grateful for gifts. Do not take on more than you can do. Remember the most valuable thing you can give is your time. Always respect the privacy and dignity of someone you are visiting.

1. Collect for the elderly and those in need
   Money to buy Christmas presents (especially food).
   Warm clothing and blankets.
   Tins of food.
   Food including some treats for Christmas hampers.

2. Knit
   something to make blankets - there is usually a local organisation already doing this - ask at your church or your doctor's surgery. These are easy and really useful at home and overseas. Knit scarves, gloves and hats. Be sure that the colours are sensible.

3. Visit - visits to establishments must always be pre-arranged. Call in to see the person in charge or phone. If it is a group or class visit confirm the arrangements in writing stating the date, time, purpose and how many will be coming. Mobile phones should be switched off again supervision is essential.
   Hospital - singing carols and play reading.
   Old People's Homes.
   The elderly in their own homes.
   Relatives.
   Elderly...

4. Help generally with
   housework
   errands
   cleaning
   gardening.

5. At home help with
   chores
   washing up
   tidying your bedroom
   making your own bed.

6. On Christmas Day
   help with the preparation of the Christmas fare.
   help to lay the house.
   make any visitors feel especially welcome
   help look after younger brothers and sisters
   help to clear up toys - people often fall over presents left on the floor.
   help to look after pets.
   be appreciative of all the work that has been done to make Christmas Day special.

WHAT I WOULD LIKE FOR CHRISTMAS

Make a list of some of the things you would like for Christmas. Give reasons for your choices. Remember that everyone likes to receive presents like toys and games but there are other things too like a visit to a special relative or a day out.

Are there any special gifts you would like to give?

Which names should go on the gift tags?

Matthew is 10 and is very keen on rugby.

Jill is three and likes to take a cuddly toy to bed with her.

Gran likes to travel, especially to see her grandchildren.

Granddad collects stamps.

Emma is 14 and likes pony trekking.

Mum would like to ride in a hot air balloon.

Dad likes fishing.

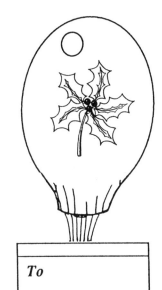

To

To

To

To

To

To

CHRISTMAS POST

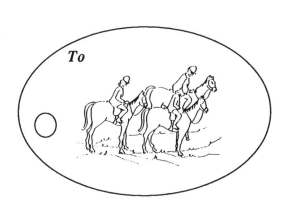

To

WHAT I WOULD LIKE FOR CHRISTMAS

Make a list of some of the things you would like for Christmas. Give reasons for your choices. Remember that everyone likes to receive presents like toys and games but there are other things too like a visit to a special relative or a day out. Are there any special gifts you would like to give?

Which names should go on the gift tags?
Matthew is 10 and is very keen on rugby.
Jill is three and likes to take a cuddly toy to bed with her.
Gran likes to travel, especially to see her grandchildren.
Grandad collects stamps.
Emma is 14 and likes pony trekking.
Mum would like to ride in a hot air balloon.
Dad likes fishing.

CHRISTMAS CRACKERS

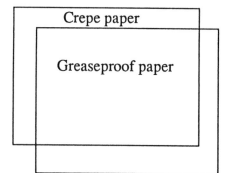

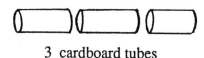

3 cardboard tubes

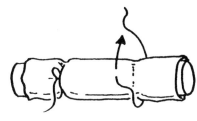

Tie with string

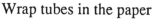

Wrap tubes in the paper

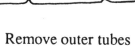

Decorate cracker

Remove outer tubes

You need
the tubes from three toilet rolls or three pieces of card 16 cm x 11 cm.
a sheet of greaseproof paper 30 cm x 21 cm.
a sheet of brightly coloured crepe paper 30 cm x 21 cm.
string, glue, six paper clips.

If you are using card, roll up each piece into a tube about the same size as the tube in a toilet roll. Glue the edges so that the pieces cannot unwind. They can be held in place with paper clips while the glue dries.
Place the sheet of greaseproof paper on top of the crepe paper on a table or desk. Place any gift or paper hat in the middle tube and lay the three tubes in a line on the sheet of greaseproof paper. Roll the greaseproof paper and the tissue paper around the three tubes. Tie with thread at both ends of the middle tube. Leave until the glue is dry (about 1 hour) then take out the outer tubes. Decorate the cracker with shiny coloured paper and pictures.

CHRISTMAS CRACKERS

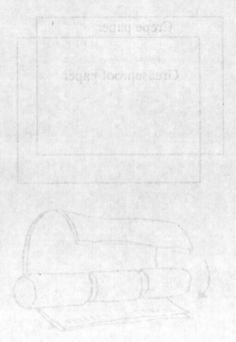

Crepe paper

Greaseproof paper

3 cardboard tubes

Tie with string

Decorate cracker

Wrap tubes in the paper.

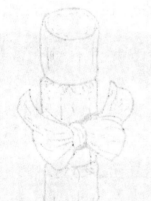

Remove outer tubes

You need

the tubes from three toilet rolls or three pieces of card 16 cm x 11 cm.
a sheet of greaseproof paper 30 cm x 21 cm.
a sheet of brightly coloured crape paper 30 cm x 21 cm.
string, glue, six paper clips.

If you are using card, roll up each piece into a tube about the same size as the tube in a toilet roll. Glue the edges so that the pieces cannot unwind. They can be held in place with paper clips while the glue dries.

Place the sheet of greaseproof paper on top of the crepe paper on a table or desk. Place any gift or paper hat in the middle tube and lay the three tubes in a line on the sheet of greaseproof paper. Roll the greaseproof paper and the tissue paper around the three tubes. Tie with thread at both ends of the middle tube. Leave until the glue is dry (about 1 hour) then take out the outer tubes. Decorate the cracker with shiny coloured paper and pictures.

SANTA CLAUS
AND HIS HELPERS

Colour this picture of Santa Claus and his helpers.

Why does Santa need helpers?

It is December 24th. and Santa is giving them instructions. What do you think he
is saying?

What do you think Santa and his helpers will do next?

SANTA CLAUS GETS READY

Colour this picture of Santa Claus loading his sleigh with presents. What will he do with all these presents?

What do you think is on the computer printout? How can you get your name on this list?

SANTA CLAUS
ON HIS SLEIGH

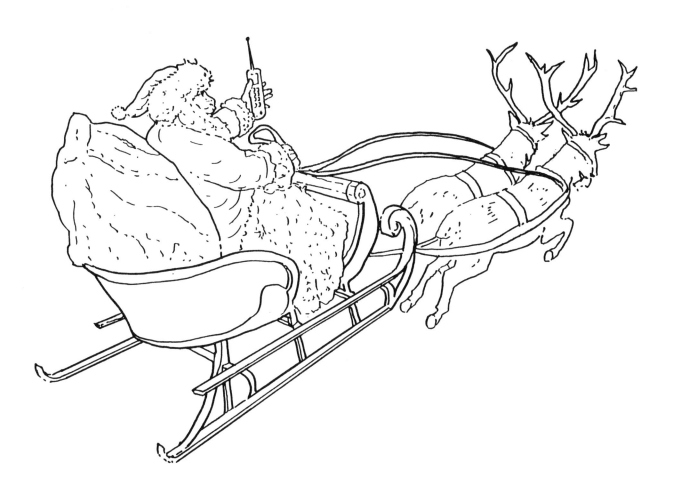

Where is Santa going? Who do you think he is talking to on his mobile phone?

Write a story beginning:

It was nearly midnight on Christmas Eve and Santa was lost . . .

SANTA CLAUS
ON HIS SLEIGH

Where is Santa going? Who do you think he is talking to on his mobile phone?

Write a story beginning:

It was nearly midnight on Christmas Eve and Santa was lost.

LET'S HAVE A PARTY

Colour this picture of a party.

Make a list of what you like to eat at a party.

If you were going to a Fancy Dress Party at Christmas, what would you wear?

Some games you might like to play. (Have small prizes for the winners.)

Pin the Tail on Mary's Donkey.

Musical Chairs using Christmas carols as the music.

Guess the adverts. (Put adverts on the wall with the names of the products removed - do not mark the wall. Check with your parents and use Blu -Tack.)

Guess my name. (Put the name of a famous person on the back of each guest. The guests ask each other questions to find out what names are on their backs.)

Give Us A Clue.

Colour this picture of a party.

Make a list of what you like to eat at a party.

If you were going to a Fancy Dress Party at Christmas, what would you wear?

Some games you might like to play. (Have small prizes for the winners.)

Pin the Tail on Mary's Donkey.

Musical Chairs using Christmas carols as the music.

Guess the adverts. (Put adverts on the wall with the names of the products removed - do not mark the wall. Check with your parents and use Blu-Tack.)

Guess my name. (Put the name of a famous person on the back of each guest. The guests ask each other questions to find out what names are on their backs.)

Give Us A Clue.

CHRISTMAS PUPPETS
CRIB

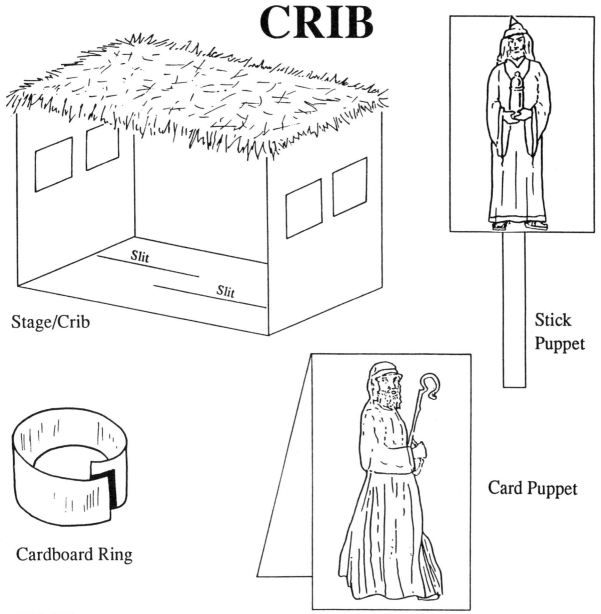

Stage/Crib

Stick Puppet

Cardboard Ring

Card Puppet

STAGE

Cover the lid of a box with straw. Cut away one side and cut slits in the bottom. There are backgrounds on page 74.

STICK PUPPETS

Colour the figures on page 73. Paste them on to cardboard and cut them out. Glue them to washed lollypop sticks. Push these sticks through the slits in the bottom of the stage and move the puppets.

FINGER PUPPETS

Make the puppets in the same way but glue each to a ring of cardboard. Put your finger in the ring to make the puppet move.

CARD PUPPETS

Paste the figures on to folded sheets of card so that they can stand up.

CRIB

Use stick puppets or make the figures for the Nativity scene out of plasticine.

CHRISTMAS PUPPETS
CRIB

Stick Puppet

Stage/Crib

Card Puppet

Cardboard Ring

STAGE
Cover the lid of a box with straw. Cut away one side and cut slits in the bottom. There are backgrounds on page 74.

STICK PUPPETS
Colour the figures on page 73. Paste them on to cardboard and cut them out. Glue them to washed lollipop sticks. Push these sticks through the slits in the bottom of the stage and move the puppets.

FINGER PUPPETS
Make the puppets in the same way, but glue each to a ring of cardboard. Put your finger in the ring to make the puppet move.

CARD PUPPETS
Paste the figures on to folded sheets of card so that they can stand up.

CRIB
Use stick puppets or make the figures for the Nativity scene out of plasticine.

Mary

Joseph

Gabriel

Three Shepherds

Servant

Innkeeper

Three Wise Men from the East

Angels

Herod

Captain of the Guard

Donkey

Baby Jesus

STAGE BACKGROUNDS

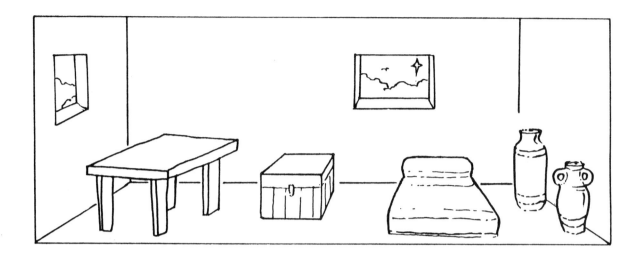

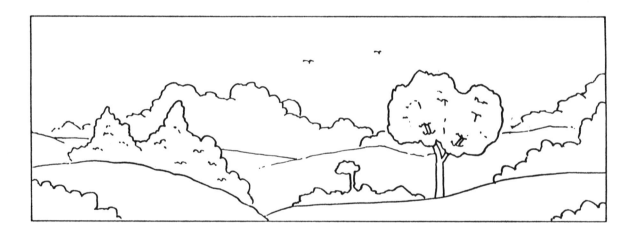

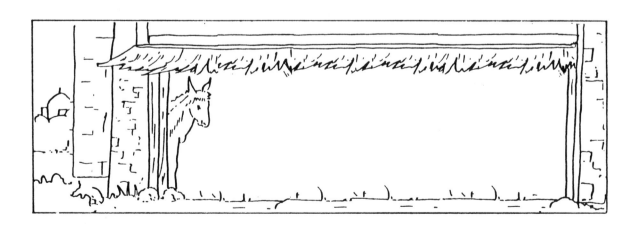

Draw and colour these backgrounds on the inside of the box stage. Use different boxes for each scene.

STAGE BACKGROUNDS

Draw and colour these backgrounds on the inside of the box stage. Use different boxes for each scene.

CHRISTMAS FRIEZE

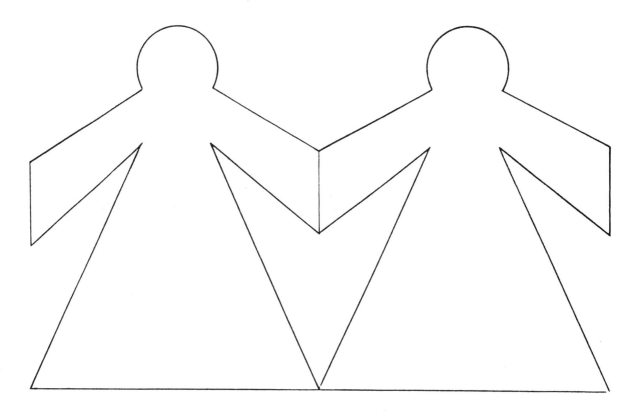

Make a line of these figures. Draw and colour the characters of the Christmas Story on them to make a frieze.

CHRISTMAS BOOKMARK

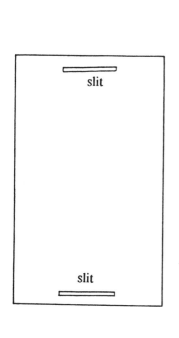

slit

slit

Cut a piece of card 20 cm long and 5 cm wide. Make two slits in it.
Paste a figure from page 73 on the card.
Thread a piece of ribbon 26 cm long through the slits.

CHRISTMAS BIRD

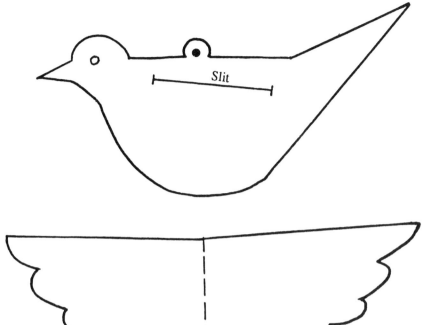

Paste the bird and its wings on to thin card and cut out.

Colour the bird. Cover the wings with glitter or stars.

Make a slit and a small hole in the bird.

Pass the wings through the slit and bend them.

Pass a thread through the hole and hang the bird on your Christmas tree.

ICE CRYSTALS

Paste the crystal on to thin card.

Colour or cover with silver glitter.

Cut out.

Pass a thread through the small hole and hang on your Christmas tree.

CHRISTMAS BORDER

CHRISTMAS ROSES

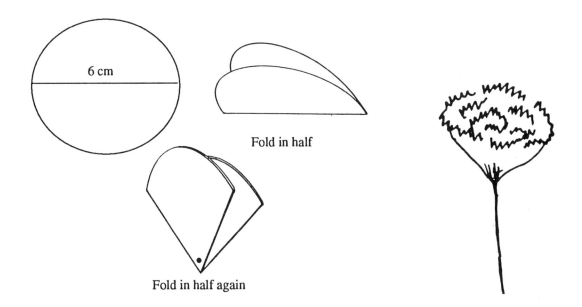

6 cm

Fold in half

Fold in half again

Cut 15 to 20 circles, diameter 6 cm, out of crepe or tissue paper. Use red, pink , white or yellow paper. The number of circles to give a full rose depends on the thickness of the paper.

Fold each circle in half and then in half again.

Using a strong sewing needle and cotton, thread the folded circles together. Pull tight and fasten the cotton.

Hang from your Christmas tree or slip a 50 cm length of florists' wire through the rose, bend the wire and twist to make a stem.

CHRISTMAS PAPER CHAINS

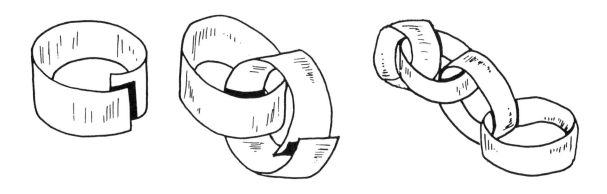

Cut some coloured strips of paper 30 cm long and 3 cm wide. Make one of the strips into a circle and glue the ends together. Thread another strip through this circle and glue the edges of the second strip together. Add more circles until the chain is long enough.

CHRISTMAS ROSES

CHRISTMAS ROSES

Fold in half

Fold in half again

Cut 5 to 20 mm leaf diameter circles out of crepe or tissue paper. Use red, pink, white or yellow paper. The number of circles to give a full rose depends on the thickness of the paper.

Fold each circle in half and then in half again.

Using a strong sewing needle and cotton, thread the folded circles together. Pull tight and fasten the cotton.

Hang from your Christmas tree or stick a 30 cm length of florist's wire through the rose, bend the wire and twist to make a stem.

CHRISTMAS PAPER CHAINS

Get some coloured strips of paper 30 cm long and 3 cm wide. Make one of the strips into a circle and glue the ends together. Thread another strip through this circle and glue the edges of the second strip together. Add more circles until the chain is long enough.

MAKE A
CHRISTMAS CANDLE

Put these directions in the correct order then make the Christmas candle.

1. Wipe any juice spilled when making the hole and tie a ribbon around the middle of the orange.

2. Push a candle into the hole.

3. Choose a large, firm orange.

4. Make sure the candle is upright.

5. Place the orange in a small dish making sure that the hole is on top and that the ribbon can be seen.

6. Finally, push the sticks into the orange.

7. Make a hole in the orange big enough to hold a candle.

8. Next thread some fruit (e g cherries and grapes) and nuts on several cocktail sticks.

[The first one is number 3.]

MAKE A
CHRISTMAS CANDLE

Put these directions in the correct order then make the Christmas candle.

1. Wipe any juice spilled when making the hole and tie a ribbon around the middle of the orange.

2. Push a candle into the hole.

3. Choose a large, firm orange.

4. Make sure the candle is upright.

5. Place the orange in a small dish and make sure that the hole is on top and that the ribbon can be seen.

6. Finally push the sticks into the orange.

7. Make a hole in the orange big enough to hold a candle.

8. Next thread some fruit (e.g. cherries and grapes) and nuts on several cocktail sticks.

[The first one is number 3.]

RUDOLF
AND DASHER, DANCER, PRANCER, VIXEN, COMET, CUPID, DONNER AND BLITZEN

Fill in the missing words.

Once upon a time there was a reindeer called Rudolf who had a very red _____ .

Every Christmas he watched Santa and his team of reindeer set off to deliver _____ to all the girls and boys.

He wished he could go with _____ .

One Christmas, there were so many parcels on Santa's _____ that Santa asked Rudolf to help.

Rudolf was delighted and his nose shone _____ than ever.

The other reindeer, Dasher, Dancer, Prancer, Vixen, Comet, Cupid, Donner and _____ liked Rudolf.

They put him in front because his nose _____ in the dark and helped them to find their way.

Watch the sky on _____ Eve for Rudolf with his bright red nose.

RUDOLF
AND DASHER, DANCER, PRANCER, VIXEN, COMET, CUPID, DONNER AND BLITZEN

Fill in the missing words.

Once upon a time there was a reindeer called Rudolf who had a very red _____.

Every Christmas he watched Santa and his team of reindeer set off to deliver _____ to all the girls and boys.

He wished he could go with _____.

One Christmas, there were so many parcels on Santa's _____ that Santa asked Rudolf to help.

Rudolf was delighted and his nose shone _____ than ever.

The other reindeer Dasher, Dancer, Prancer, Vixen, Comet, Cupid, Donner and _____ liked Rudolf.

They put him in front because his nose _____ in the dark and helped them to find their way.

Watch the sky on _____ Eve for Rudolf with his bright red nose.

PUZZLES

Put these snowmen in ascending order of size,
beginning with the smallest.

On Christmas Eve Joseph was waiting for
Santa Claus to bring him his presents.
Suddenly, he heard a noise in the chimney
and Santa's foot appeared. There were
wriggling noises and a cross voice
said,'This chimney is too small . . .
Write a story called 'The Night Santa was
stuck in the Chimney.'

Which two Santas are the same?

Put these snowmen in ascending order of size, beginning with the smallest.

On Christmas Eve Joseph was waiting for Santa Claus to bring him his presents. Suddenly, he heard a noise in the chimney and Santa's foot appeared. There were wriggling noises and a cross voice said, "This chimney is too small." Which a story called The Night Santa was stuck in the Chimney.

Which two Santas are the same?

CHRISTMAS MAZE

A
B
C
D

Which path must Santa Claus follow to reach the house?

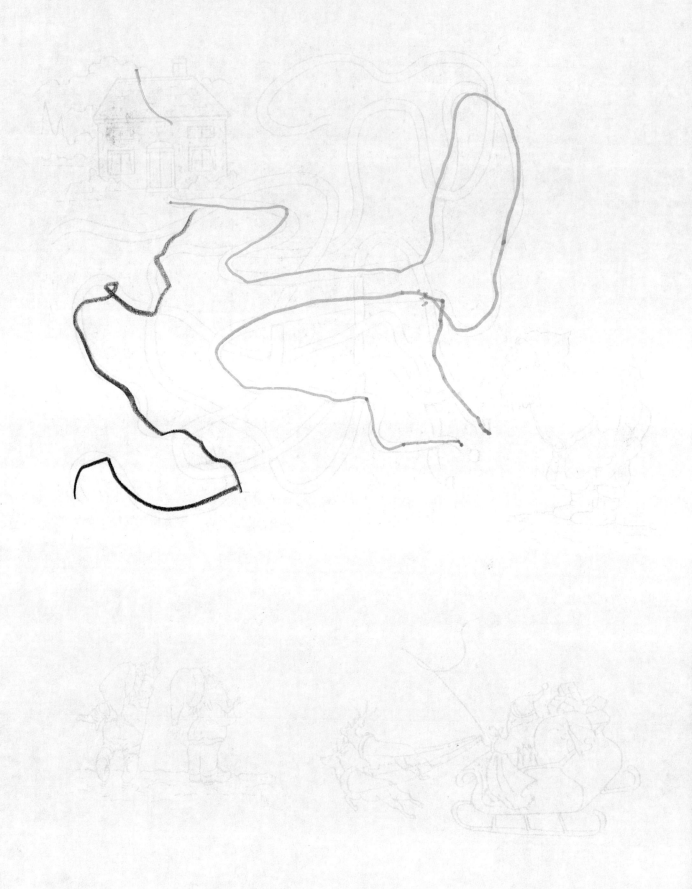

Which path must Santa Claus follow to reach the house?

Find ten differences between these two pictures.

Find ten differences between these two pictures.

SAVOURY ROLLS

Crusty rolls with savoury butters and fillings make delicious snacks.
Use different kinds of white and brown rolls. Cut open or in half. Butter and fill.

Savoury butters

Mix creamed butter with any of the following: anchovy paste, cheese, chopped chives, mashed hard boiled egg, tomato ketchup, chopped cooked prawns, salmon paste, sardines, watercress.

Fillings

Cream cheese, chopped chives and spring onions
Cucumber slices
Meat spread
Sweet pickles and cheese
Chopped cooked chicken with stuffing
Chopped pork with sage and onion stuffing
Prawn with mayonnaise
Mixed salad

BEEFBURGERS

Ingredients

500 g lean minced beef
$\frac{1}{2}$ teaspoon Worcestershire sauce
Pinch of salt
Pinch of freshly ground black pepper
4 baps
Lettuce
Large tomato
Cucumber
Large onion
Chutney or ketchup

Method

Wash the lettuce and tomato. Slice the tomato and cucumber. Skin and slice the onion.

Turn on the grill to warm.

Put the minced beef in a bowl. Add the Worcestershire sauce, salt and pepper. Mix well.

Divide the meat into four and shape into four flat rounds about 1 cm thick.

Put the beefburgers under the grill for 3 to 5 minutes.

Using kitchen tongs, turn the beefburgers over to cook the other side.

Cut open the baps. Put the beefburgers in the baps with the lettuce, onion, cucumber and tomato slices.

Serve with chutney or ketchup and more salad.

SAVOURY ROLLS

Savoury rolls with savoury butters and fillings make a delicious snack.

Use different kinds of white and brown rolls. Cut open or in half. Butter and fill.

Savoury butters

Mix creamed butter with any of the following: anchovy paste, cheese, chopped chives, mashed hard boiled egg, tomato ketchup, chopped cooked prawns, salmon paste, sardines, water cress.

Fillings

Cream cheese, chopped chives and spring onions

Cucumber slices

Meat spread

Sweet pickles and cheese

Chopped cooked chicken with stuffing

Chopped pork with sage and onion stuffing

Prawn with mayonnaise

Mixed salad

BEEFBURGERS

Ingredients

500 g lean minced beef

1 tbsp. Worcestershire sauce

Pinch of salt

Pinch of freshly ground black pepper

4 baps

Lettuce

Large tomato

Cucumber

Large onion

Chutney or ketchup

Method

Wash the lettuce and tomato. Slice the tomato and cucumber. Skin and slice the onion.

Turn the grill to warm.

Put the minced beef in a bowl. Add the Worcestershire sauce, salt and pepper.

Mix well.

Divide the meat into four and shape into four flat rounds about 1 cm thick.

Put the beefburgers under the grill for 3 to 5 minutes.

Using kitchen tongs, turn the beefburgers over to cook the other side.

Cut open the baps. Put the beefburgers in the baps with the lettuce, onion, cucumber and tomato slices.

Serve with chutney or ketchup and room salad.

TRUFFLES

Ingredients

100 g plain chocolate

50 g caster sugar

50 g cake crumbs (stale cake is fine)

2 tablespoons Coca Cola

2 tablespoons apricot jam

50 g chocolate bits (or crushed Flake)

Method

Soak the cake crumbs in the Coca Cola. Stand a basin in a bowl of hot water. Break the plain chocolate into pieces in the basin and melt the chocolate. Remove the basin from the water and beat in the sugar and cake crumbs. When the mixture is cool, form into small balls. Coat with apricot jam and dip in chocolate bits or crushed Flake.

CHRISTMAS PUNCH

Ingredients

500 g mixed fruits - strawberries, raspberries, grapes, oranges, apples

500 ml unsweetened apple juice

500 ml orange juice

500 ml lemonade

Method

Wash the fruit. Peel and slice the oranges and apples. Put into a large bowl and add the liquids. Stir. Serve in tall glasses with ice.

TRUFFLES

Ingredients
100 g plain chocolate
50 g caster sugar
50 g cake crumbs (stale cake is fine)
2 tablespoons Coca Cola
2 tablespoons apricot jam
50 g chocolate bits (or crushed Flake)

Method
Soak the cake crumbs in the Coca Cola. Stand a basin in a bowl of hot water. Break the plain chocolate into pieces in the basin and melt the chocolate. Remove the basin from the water and beat in the sugar and cake crumbs. When the mixture is cool, form into small balls. Coat with apricot jam and dip in chocolate bits or crushed Flake.

CHRISTMAS PUNCH

Ingredients
500 g mixed fruits - strawberries, raspberries, grapes, oranges, apples
500 ml unsweetened apple juice
500 ml orange juice
500 ml lemonade

Method
Wash the fruit. Peel and slice the oranges and apples. Put into a large bowl and add the liquids. Stir. Serve in tall glasses with ice.

HOLLY TRIMMED SCARF

Materials

100 g double knitting yarn in white.
Small amounts of double knitting yarn in dark green and red.
1 pair 4.5 mm knitting needles.

Abbreviations

X Dark green yarn (G)
* Bright red yarn (R)
W and all other stitches white
st stitch, sts stitches, st. st. stocking stich, K knit, P purl.

Method

Cast on 45 sts.
Work 6 rows in rib, K1 P1.
Work in garter stitch until it is long enough.
Work 6 rows in rib, Ki P1
Cast off.

Holly Motif. Work two.

Follow the chart to knit or to embroider the holly in cross stitch.
The motif is worked in stocking stitch. K odd numbered rows, reading from right to left and P even numbered rows, reading from left to right.

Twist the yarns when changing colours.
Cast on 15 sts and work 2 rows in st.st.

Chart

Row 1 K 7W, 1R, 7W.
Row 2 P 6W, 3R, 6W
Row 3 K 3W, 1G, (1W, 1R) 3 times, 1W, 1G, 3W
Row 4 P 3W 1G, 2W, 1R, 1G, 1R, 2W, 1G, 3W
Row 5 K 4W, 7G, 4W
Row 6 P 4W, 7G, 4W
Row 7 K 3W, 9G, 3W
Row 8 P 5W, 5G, 5W
Row 9 K 3W, 9G, 3W
Row 10 P 2W, 11G, 2W
Row 11 K 4W, 7G, 4W
Row 12 P 5W, 5G, 5W
Row 13 K 6W, 3G, 6W
Row 14 P 6W, 3G, 6W
Row 15 K 7W, 1G, 7W
Row 16 P 7W, 1G, 7W
Work 2 rows in st. st.
Cast off.
Sew a holly panel at each end of the scarf.

HOLLY CHART

CROSS STITCH

Row	1	2	3	4	5	6	7	8	9	10	11
16						X					
15						X					
14					X	X	X				
13					X	X	X				
12				X	X	X	X	X			
11			X	X	X	X	X	X	X		
10	X	X	X	X	X	X	X	X	X	X	X
9		X	X	X	X	X	X	X	X	X	
8				X	X	X	X	X			
7		X	X	X	X	X	X	X	X	X	
6			X	X	X	X	X	X	X		
5			X	X	X	X	X	X	X		
4		X	W	W	*	X	*	W	W	X	
3		X	W	*	W	*	W	*	W	X	
2					*	*	*				
1						*					

PUZZLES

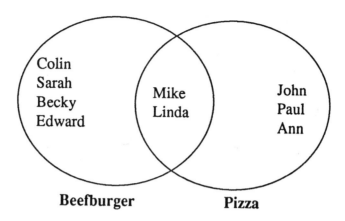

Beefburger   **Pizza**

8 children went to a party. Who ate a beefburger only? Who ate pizza only?
Who ate a beefburger and pizza?

Ann bought three Christmas cards at 54p each and three stamps at 24p each.
How much change did she have from £2.50?

Find the numbers missing from the boxes.

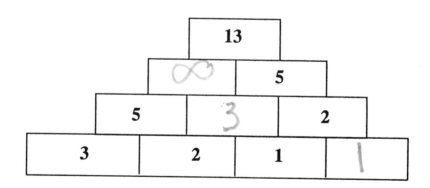

Clue: The two numbers below add up to the one in the row above, for example,
in the bottom row, 3+2 = 5 in the row above.

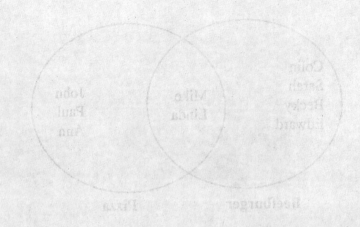

8 children went to a party. Who ate beefburger only? Who ate pizza only?

Who ate beefburger and pizza?

Ann bought three Christmas cards at 30p each and three stamps at 24p each.

How much change did she have from £2.50?

Find the numbers missing from the boxes.

Clue: The two numbers below add up to the one in the row above, for example,

in the bottom row, 3+2=5 in the row above.

PUZZLES

There are 12 words on the Christmas tree but their letters are muddled. Can you find them?

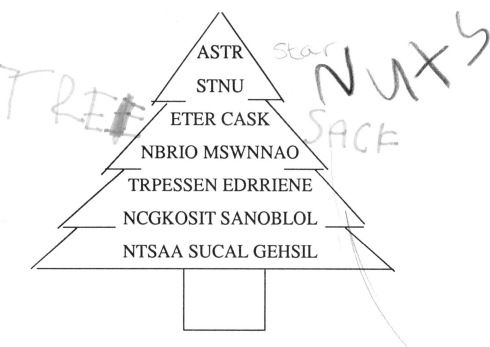

ASTR
STNU
ETER CASK
NBRIO MSWNNAO
TRPESSEN EDRRIENE
NCGKOSIT SANOBLOL
NTSAA SUCAL GEHSIL

After the first few words, the spaces between the words in the following passage are in the wrong places. Can you put them in the correct places?

THE SHEPHERDS AND THE ANGELS

The shepherds in the fields around Bethlehemwe rewatc hing theirshe ep asth eyal waysd id. Sud denly, an an gelapp ea red. Theshe pherdswe reter rifiedb utthean gelsaid, 'Don'tbe fri ght ened. I ha vecome wi thgood ne wsfory ou. Itwill br ingjoy tot he who leworld. A ba bywas bo rnin Bethle hem. Heis Christthe Lo rd! Goand seeh imfo ryou rselves. Youw ill findh imw rapped inswad dling clo thes andly ing ina man ger.' Theshep herds race dac rossthe fieldsa nd at lastfound Jos ephand Mary witht hebabyas leepast heangel ha dsa idthe ywo uld.

PUZZLES

There are 12 words on the Christmas tree but their letters are muddled. Can you find them?

After the first few words, the speaker... can the words in the following passage are in the wrong places. Can you put them in the correct place?

THE SHEPHERDS AND THE ANGELS

The shepherds in the fields around Bethlehem were watching their sheep each eve...

PUZZLES

Below the square are clues to words hidden in the word square. Can you find the hidden words?

The words may be in the square backwards, upside down or diagonally and any letter may be used once only, more than once or not at all.

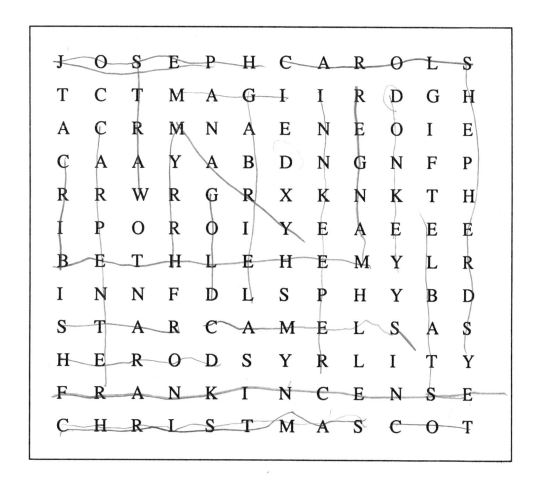

```
J O S E P H C A R O L S
T C T M A G I I R D G H
A C R M N A E N E O I E
C A A Y A B D N G N F P
R R W R G R X K N K T H
I P O R O I Y E A E E E
B E T H L E H E M Y L R
I N N F D L S P H Y B D
S T A R C A M E L S A S
H E R O D S Y R L I T Y
F R A N K I N C E N S E
C H R I S T M A S C O T
```

1. Festival to celebrate the birth of Jesus.
2. Mother of Jesus.
3. Married to Mary.
4. Angel who visited Mary and told her she was going to have a very special baby.
5. Left their sheep to look for Jesus.
6. The three wise men.
7/8/9. Gifts brought to Jesus by the three wise men.
10. City where Jesus was born.
11. A sign in the sky that showed where Jesus would be born.
12. The wise men rode on these.

13. Mary rode to Bethlehem on this.
14. Man who said there was no room at the inn.
15. Room in which Jesus was born.
16. Babies usually sleep in this.
17. Jesus slept in this.
18. Used to keep Jesus warm.
19. Used today to show how baby Jesus slept in the stable.
20. Jesus grew up as a carpenter like his earthly father.
21. King who wanted to kill the infant Jesus.
22. Songs sung at Christmas.

PUZZLES

Below the square are clues to words hidden in the word square. Can you find the hidden words?

The words may be in the square backwards, upside down or diagonally and any letter may be used once only, more than once or not at all.

```
I O S E P H C A R O L E S
T C T M A G I I R D C H
A R M N A E N L S O I E
C A A Y A B D N G N T P
H B S L Z A K N K T H
T P O K O H Y E A I E E
B E T N L E H E R M Y U R
I N N P D I S P H Y B T
S T A R C A M E L S A S
H E R O D S Y R L I T Y
F R A N K I N C E N S E
C H R I S T M A S C O T
```

1. Festival to celebrate the birth of Jesus.
2. Mother of Jesus.
3. Married to Mary.
4. Angel who visited Mary and told her she was going to have a very special baby.
5. Left their sheep to look for Jesus.
6. The three wise men.
7. Gifts brought to Jesus by the three wise men.
10. City where Jesus was born.
11. A sign in the sky that showed where Jesus would be born.
12. The wise men rode on these.

13. Mary rode to Bethlehem on this.
14. Man who said there was no room at the inn.
15. Room in which Jesus was born.
16. Babies usually sleep in this.
17. Jesus slept in this.
18. Used to keep Jesus warm.
19. Used today to show how baby Jesus slept in the table.
20. Jesus grew up as a - - - - - - - - like his earthly father.
21. King who wanted to kill the infant Jesus.
22. Songs sung at Christmas.

Shhhh! No E I P E A D E ?

A CHRISTMAS QUIZ

1. Name the town where Joseph and Mary lived.

2. Name the angel who visited Mary to tell her about the birth of Jesus.

3. What is a census?

4. Name the town to which Mary and Joseph travelled just before the birth of Jesus. Why did they go there?

5. Name the three shepherds who came to look for baby Jesus.

6. What did the angel tell the shepherds to follow?

7. Why was baby Jesus born in a stable?

8. Name the town where Jesus was born.

9. Who was king when Jesus was born?

10. Name the three wise men. What gifts did they bring to the infant Jesus?

11. Why did the three wise men decide not to tell Herod where Jesus was?

12. Do you think the wise men were correct not to tell Herod about Jesus? Why?

13. What do French children leave by the fire on Christmas Eve?

14. What do the Poles call Christmas Eve?

15. When do Dutch people celebrate Christmas?

16. Who was Father Christmas?

17. Who or what are Dasher, Dancer, Prancer, Donner and Blitzen?

18. What do you understand by 'Advent'?

20. What is meant by 'Epiphany'?

20. What do Scots call New Year's Eve?

21. Who invented Christmas crackers?

22. Where does the name 'Boxing Day' come from?

23. When was the first Christmas card produced?

24. When and where did the custom of decorating the Christmas tree begin?

25. Who decided 25 December should be Christmas Day?

A CHRISTMAS QUIZ

1. Name the town where Joseph and Mary lived.

2. Name the angel who visited Mary to tell her about the birth of Jesus.

3. What is a census?

4. Name the town to which Mary and Joseph travelled just before the birth of Jesus. Why did they go there?

5. Name the three shepherds who came to look for baby Jesus.

6. What did the angel tell the shepherds to follow?

7. Why was baby Jesus born in a stable?

8. Name the town where Jesus was born.

9. Who was king when Jesus was born?

10. Name the three wise men. What gifts did they bring to the infant Jesus?

11. Why did the three wise men decide not to tell Herod where Jesus was?

12. Do you think the wise men were correct not to tell Herod about Jesus? Why?

13. Where do French children leave by the fire on Christmas Eve?

14. What do the Poles call Christmas Eve?

15. When do Dutch people celebrate Christmas?

16. Who was Father Christmas?

17. Who or what are Dasher, Dancer, Prancer, Donner and Blitzen?

18. What do you understand by 'Advent'?

19. What is meant by 'Epiphany'?

20. What do Scots call New Year's Eve?

21. Who invented Christmas crackers?

22. Where does the name Boxing Day come from?

23. When was the first Christmas card produced?

24. When and where did the custom of decorating the Christmas tree begin?

25. Who decided 25 December should be Christmas Day?

PICK A LETTER

For two or more players.

Paste the letter sheet on to the card from a cereal box and cut out the squares. Place them face down on the table. The card ? can be any letter.

There are two ways in which the game can be played, one is a little simpler than the other.

QUICK AND SIMPLE

Each player turns over a letter until he or she can make a word. The word is then picked up and placed in front of the player. Score 1 point for each letter in the word. The other players continue to turn the letter cards over. The game finishes when all the cards have been turned over and the player with the most points wins.

For example: Suppose

Player 1 turns over letter A.

Player 2 turns over letter T.

Player 3 turns over letter F and makes the word FAT scoring 3 points and placing the word in front of him or her.

A LITTLE HARDER

If you wish you may also use words already made by you or other players.

Suppose Player 4 turns over Letter E, takes the word FAT and makes FATE scoring 4 points and placing the word in front of him or her.

Player 1 turns over the letter S and takes the letters FATE and makes FEAT (4 points) then FEATS, then FATES, then FEAST scoring 4 + 5 + 5 + 5 = 19 points.

You can of course make extra letter cards to make the game last longer. Only words found in a good dictionary can be accepted.

[Rules can vary, for example, smallest word accepted must have four letters, no plurals allowed. . . Agree how the game is to be played before you start.]

NB If the letters of a word can be re-arranged to make another word then it is an ANAGRAM. Therefore FEAT is an anagram of FATE.

PICK A LETTER

For two or more players.

Paste the letter sheet on to the card from a cereal box and cut out on the squares. Place them face down on the table. The card ? can be any letter.

There are two ways in which the game can be played, one is a little simpler than the other.

QUICK AND SIMPLE

Each player turns over a letter until he or she can make a word. The word is then picked up and placed in front of the player. Score 1 point for each letter in the word. The other players continue to turn the letter cards over. The game finishes when all the cards have been turned over and the player with the most points wins.

For example: Suppose

Player 1 turns over a letter A

Player 2 turns over letter T

Player 3 turns over letter F and makes the word FAT scoring 3 points and placing the word in front of him or her.

A LITTLE HARDER

If you wish you may also use words already made by you or other players.

Suppose Player 4 turns over letter E takes the word FAT and makes FATE scoring 4 points and placing the word in front of him or her.

Player 1 turns over the letter S and takes the letters FATE and makes FEATS (4 points) they FEATS, then FATES, then FEAST scoring 4 + 5 + 5 + 5 = 19 points.

You can of course make extra letter cards to make the game last longer. Only words found in a good dictionary can be accepted.

[Rules can vary, for example, smallest word accepted must have four letters, no plurals allowed... Agree how the game is to be played before you start.]

NB If the letters of a word can be re-arranged to make another word then it is an ANAGRAM. Therefore FRAT from anagram of FATE.

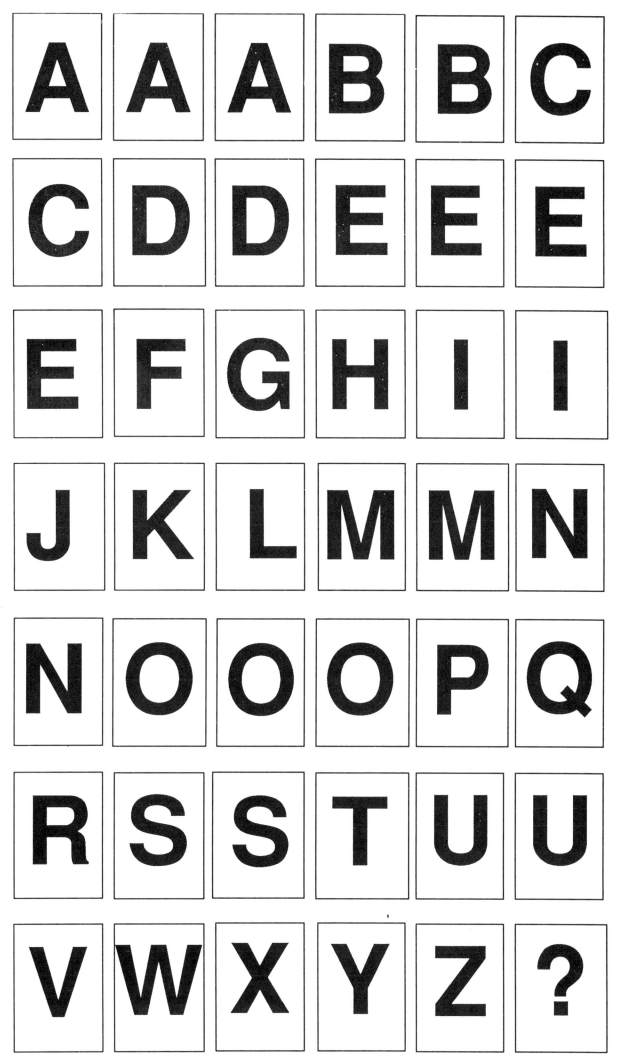

CARD GAMES

Colour the picture cards on this sheet so that the ones with the same picture are coloured alike. Paste the sheets on cardboard from a large cereal box and cut out the cards. **You will have four of each kind - four of the three wise men, four churches and so on.** There is a Father Christmas picture for the back of each card.

CHRISTMAS SNAP

For two or more players.

Shuffle the cards and deal them all out face down. The players hold their cards face down so that they cannot be seen. The player to the left of the dealer places a card face up on the table. In turn, each player places a card face up on top of this. When two cards with the same picture follow each other, the player who first shouts SNAP picks up the cards on the table. The winner is the one with all the cards.

MIX AND MATCH

The aim of the game is to find pairs of identical pictures. The pack of cards is shuffled and the dealer lays out the pack face down on a table or on the floor. The person to the left of the dealer turns over two cards. If they are the same, he or she keeps them and has another turn, if not the cards are turned face down again. The person to the left then picks up two cards and so on. As more cards are turned over and replaced, it is possible to remember which are pairs. The winner is the player with the most pairs. This can also be played by one person who sets a target time by which all the cards must be paired.

CARD GAMES

Colour the picture cards on this sheet so that the ones with the same picture are coloured alike. Paste the sheets on cardboard from a large cereal box and cut out the cards. You will have four of each kind – four of the three wise men, four churches and so on. There is a Father Christmas picture for the back of each card.

CHRISTMAS SNAP

For two or more players.

Shuffle the cards and deal them all out face down. The players hold their cards face down so that they cannot be seen. The player to the left of the dealer places a card face up on the table. In turn, each player places a card face up on top of this. When two cards with the same picture follow each other, the player who first shouts SNAP picks up the cards on the table. The winner is the one with all the cards.

MIX AND MATCH

The aim of the game is to find pairs of identical pictures. The pack of cards is shuffled and the dealer lays out the pack face down on a table or on the floor. The person to the left of the dealer turns over two cards. If they are the same, he or she keeps them and has another turn, if not the cards are turned face down again. The person to the left then picks up two cards and so on. As more cards are turned over and replaced, it is possible to remember which are pairs. The winner is the player with the most pairs. This can also be played by one person who sets a target time by which all the cards must be paired.

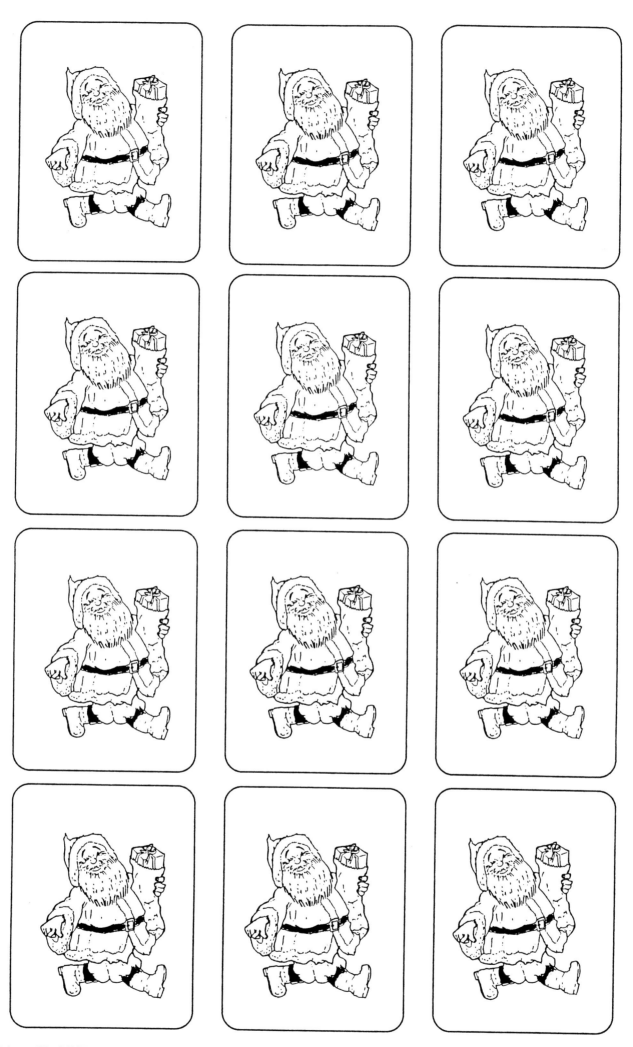

31

30

Hear about Mary and Joseph travelling to Bethlehem. Have another turn. **32**

33

Hear about the birth of baby Jesus. Have another turn. **34**

Hear about the three wise men. Have another turn. **35**

FINISH

Hear about the angels and the shepherds. Go to 31. **29**

28

Hear about the angel's visit to Mary. Go to 30. **27**

Go to church on Christmas Eve. Go to 28. **26**

25

24

Look for Father Christmas in the sky. Have another turn. **23**

Forget lines in Nativity Play. Go back to 18. **22**

15

14

Reindeer lost. Miss a turn. **16**

Snows in the night. Miss a turn. **17**

18

Build a snowman. Have another turn. **19**

Snowman melts. Go back to 18. **20**

Help to wrap presents. Have another turn. **21**

Help Father Christmas who is stuck in the chimney. Go to 15. **13**

12

Visit Father Christmas. Have another turn. **11**

10

Lights on Christmas tree go out. Go back to 5. **9**

Help to decorate Christmas Tree. Have another turn. **8**

7

Help to put up Christmas decorations. Go to 10. **6**

START

Late posting your Christmas cards. Miss a turn. **1**

Help make Christmas Pudding. Have another turn. **2**

3

Forget to ice Christmas cake. Miss a turn. **4**

5

GETTING READY FOR CHRISTMAS

Colour this game sheet using crayons or felt-tipped pens. Paste it on to thin card such as the back of a cereal packet. You need a *die.

Colour the figures, cut them out and put them at the start.

The player to throw the highest number begins then the player with the next highest number and so on. In the game, move the figures the number of squares indicated by the die.

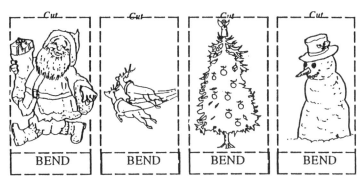

Cut — BEND Cut — BEND Cut — BEND Cut — BEND

*NB The singular of dice is die.

Christmas File © EJ P & DC P

Getting Ready for Christmas Game 95

ANSWERS

There may be correct or acceptable alternative answers.

Christmas Candle (page79)
3,7,1,5,2,4,8,6

Rudolf (page 81) nose, presents, Santa
(them), brighter, Blitzen, shone, Christmas.

Puzzles (page 81) Snowmen - C, B, D, E, A.
Santas C and E are the same.

Maze (page 82) Path C.
Puzzles (page 87) Beefburger only - Colin,
Sarah, Becky and Edward. Pizza only - John,
Paul, Ann. Beefburger and pizza - Mike and
Linda.
Ann's change = 16p.
Missing numbers.

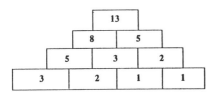

Words on the Christmas tree (page 88)
Star, Nuts, Tree, Sack, Robin, Snowman,
Presents, Reindeer, Stocking, Balloons,
Santa Claus, Sleigh.

Ten Differences page 83

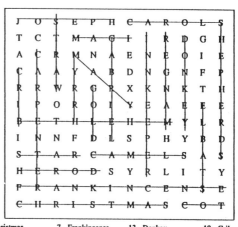

1. Christmas	7. Frankincense	13. Donkey	19. Crib
2. Mary	8. Myrrh	14. Innkeeper	20. Carpenter
3. Joseph	9. Gold	15. Stable	21. Herod
4. Gabriel	10. Bethlehem	16. Cot	22. Carols
5. Shepherds	11. Star	17. Manger	
6. Magi	12. Camels	18. Straw	

Wordsquare (page 89)

The shepherds and the angels (p 88)

The shepherds in the fields around Bethlehem were watching their sheep as they always did. Suddenly, an angel appeared. The shepherds were terrified but the angel said, 'Don't be frightened. I have come with good news for you. It will bring joy to the whole world. A baby was born in Bethlehem. He is Christ the Lord! Go and see him for yourselves. You will find him wrapped in swaddling clothes and lying in a manger.' The shepherds raced across the fields and at last found Joseph and Mary with the baby asleep as the angel had said they would.

Quiz (Page 90)

1. Nazareth in Galilee.
2. Gabriel.
3. A count of the number of people living in a particular place at a given time.
4. Bethlehem. To register in a census ordered by the Roman Emperor Augustus.
5. Matthew, Isaac and Benjamin.
6. A star.
7. Bethlehem was crowded because so many people had returned to take part in the census. There was no room at the inn.
8. Bethlehem.
9. Herod.
10. Melchior - gold,
    Caspar - frankincense,
    Balthazar - myrrh.
11. They all had the same dream warning them not to tell Herod about the birth of Jesus and where He was.
12. Yes. Herod was known to be cruel and later he ordered all male children aged two or less to be killed.
13. Their shoes.
14. The Festival of the Star.
15. On St. Nicholas Day, 6th. December.
16. A Christian bishop named Nicholas who lived in the 3rd. or 4th. century.
17. Santa's reindeer.
18. The season leading up to Christmas including four Sundays.
19. The time (6th. January) when the wise men brought their gifts to Jesus.
20. Hogmanay.
21. Tom Smith, a baker.
22. The dole of the Chrismas box, a custom from the Middle Ages when alms boxes were placed in churches at Christmas to collect money for the poor.
23. 1846.
24. Germany. An English missionary, St. Boniface, started the custom in the 8th. century.
25. Pope Gregory in 354 AD.

NATIONAL CURRICULUM

MASTER FILE

MASTER FILES

published by
Domino Books (Wales) Ltd.

AN ESTABLISHED SERIES
prepared by experienced teachers

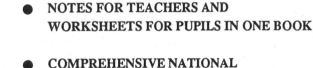

MASTER FILE MATHEMATICS KEY STAGE 2

MASTER FILE ENGLISH KEY STAGE 2

MASTER FILE SCIENCE KEY STAGE 2

MASTER FILE INVADERS AND SETTLERS THE CELTS KEY STAGE 2

MASTER FILE INVADERS AND SETTLERS THE ROMANS KEY STAGE 2

MASTER FILE LIFE IN TUDOR TIMES KEY STAGE 2

MASTER FILE INVADERS AND SETTLERS THE VIKINGS KEY STAGE 2

MASTER FILE VICTORIAN BRITAIN KEY STAGE 2

MASTER FILE

- NOTES FOR TEACHERS AND WORKSHEETS FOR PUPILS IN ONE BOOK

- COMPREHENSIVE NATIONAL CURRICULUM COVERAGE

- THERE IS NO NEED TO BUY ADDITIONAL MATERIAL

- ALL THE MATERIAL IS PHOTOCOPIABLE

- EXCELLENT VALUE

- SAVES YOU TIME AND MONEY

- VISUALLY STIMULATING

- BOOKS SPECIFICALLY DESIGNED FOR THE KEY STAGE YOU TEACH

- FULL OF TEACHING STRATEGIES AND IDEAS

- READY-TO-USE LESSONS

- FLEXIBLE RESOURCES FOR USE BY THE WHOLE CLASS, BY GROUPS OR BY INDIVIDUAL PUPILS

- TRIED AND TESTED MATERIALS

- PHOTOCOPIABLE SHEETS TO USE AS THEY ARE OR TO REDUCE OR ENLARGE

- PHOTOCOPIABLE RECORD SHEETS FOR EACH PU[PIL]

- NEW TITLES PUBLISHED MONTHLY

MASTER FILE MATHEMATICS KEY STAGE 1

MASTER FILE ENGLISH KEY STAGE 1

MASTER FILE SCIENCE KEY STAGE 1

MASTER FILE HISTORY KEY STAGE 1

First Steps Number & Counting

AVAILABLE FROM
Domino Books (Wales) Ltd.,
P O Box 32, Swansea SA1 1FN.
Tel. (01792) 459378   Fax. (01792) 466337
Telephone and fax orders welcome

MASTER FILES
ORDER FORM

KEY STAGE 1 (Age 5 - 7)   **KEY STAGE 2 (Age 7 - 11)**   **KEY STAGE 3 (Age 11 - 14)**

Quantity	Title	ISBN	Price	Cost
	MATHEMATICS (KS1)	1 85772 107 1	£20.00	£
	HISTORY (KS1)	1 85772 112 8	£20.00	£
	ENGLISH (KS1)	1 85772 111 X	£20.00	£
	SCIENCE (KS1)	1 85772 108 X	£20.00	£
	MATHEMATICS (KS2)	1 85772 086 5	£20.00	£
	ENGLISH (KS2)	1 85772 085 7	£20.00	£
	SCIENCE (KS2)	1 85772 087 3	£20.00	£
	MATHEMATICS (KS3)	1 85772 126 8	£20.00	£
	ENGLISH (KS3)	1 85772 127 6	£20.00	£
	SCIENCE (KS3)	1 85772 128 4	£20.00	£
HISTORY				
	Invaders and Settlers - The Celts (KS2)	1 85772 067 9	£15.95	£
	Invaders and Settlers - The Romans (KS2)	1 85772 070 9	£15.95	£
	Invaders and Settlers - Anglo-Saxons (KS2)	1 85772 068 7	£15.95	£
	Invaders and Settlers - The Vikings (KS2)	1 85772 069 5	£15.95	£
	Life in Tudor Times (KS2)	1 85772 076 8	£15.95	£
	Victorian Britain (KS2 - KS3)	1 85772 077 6	£15.95	£
	The Second World War (KS2 - KS3)	1 85772 121 7	£15.95	£
	The Twentieth Century World (KS2 - KS3)	1 85772 074 1	£15.95	£
TOPICS				
	Castles (KS2 - KS3)	1 85772 075 X	£15.95	£
	Christmas (Ages 5 - 12)	1 85772 065 2	£20.00	£
NEW FOR EARLY YEARS				
	First Steps (Basic Activities in the 3Rs)	1 85772 130 6	£12.50	£
	First Steps (Number and Counting)	1 85772 133 0	£12.50	
	First Steps (Beginning to Write)	1 85772 139 X	£12.50	£
	First Steps (Beginning to Read)	1 85772 138 1	£12.50	£
		Total	**£**	

Name/Organisation/School

Address

Post Code   Tel.

Contact   Signature

Order Number   Date

Available from Foyles Bookshop, Welsh Books Council, Blackwells, Georges, Bookland, Dillons, Hammicks, Waterstones, Smith and all good booksellers or direct from

DOMINO BOOKS (WALES) LTD, P O BOX 32, SWANSEA SA1 1FN
TEL. 01792 459378   FAX. 01792 466337

orders must have an official requisition form attached (schools, educational establishments, LEAs, bookshops, with private orders please.